Abd Samad Moussaoui is a teacher in a technical high school in the south of France. Florence Bouquillat, his co-writer, is a TV journalist at France 2.

ZACARIAS MOUSSAOUI
The Making of a Terrorist

Abd Samad Moussaoui
Florence Bouquillat

Translated by Simon Pleasance & Fronza Woods

A complete catalogue record for this book can
be obtained from the British Library on request.

First published in 2003 by Serpent's Tail,
4 Blackstock Mews, London N4 2BT
website: www.serpentstail.com

First published in 2002 as
Zacarias Moussaoui, mon frère
by Éditions Denoël, Paris

Printed by Mackays of Chatham, plc

10 9 8 7 6 5 4 3 2 1

CONTENTS

A NOTE FROM THE EDITOR OF THE FRENCH EDITION

Zacarias Moussaoui is Abd Samad Moussaoui's younger brother.

Zacarias Moussaoui is currently being held in a United States prison on six charges stemming from the attacks of September 11th 2001. Four of these charges are capital offences, punishable by death. As of this writing, he is the only person to be charged in connection with those attacks.

In a letter written to his mother from his prison cell, Zacarias Moussaoui wrote: 'As far as American history is concerned, I haven't done anything wrong and I shall prove as much when the time comes *in shah Allah* [...]. I am patiently awaiting the moment to prove my innocence.'[1]

He is accused of preparing acts of terrorism, and of conspiring with a view to hijacking an aircraft, destroying an aircraft, using weapons of mass destruction, murdering American officials and destroying property. A federal prosecutor is duly making moves to demand the death penalty for this French citizen, based on the allegation that Zacarias Moussaoui was involved in planning and preparing murderous attacks on United States territory.

The presumption is being made that Zacarias Moussaoui was the famous 'twentieth hijacker', the one who should have been on board one of the suicide aeroplanes on September 11th 2001 – the flight that crashed in a field in Pennsylvania.

On that particular day, Zacarias Moussaoui was behind

bars in a Shelburne County jail in Minnesota, where he had spent the past twenty-five days.

According to the American authorities, up until his arrest on 16 August 2001 Zacarias Moussaoui had been attending pilots' courses at the PanAm International Flight Academy, near Minneapolis in Minnesota. One of his instructors, a former air-force officer, had apparently found his behaviour suspicious and alerted the police.

But if we stick to the facts, Zacarias Moussaoui was arrested first and foremost for a problem to do with his 'irregular status and working illegally'. So he was first charged and then placed in detention for being in breach of the immigration laws.

He had arrived in the United States at Chicago airport on 23 February 2001, travelling on French passport number AE27016. But Zacarias Moussaoui was actually only authorized to remain in the United States for ninety-six days, until 22 May 2001. There was another detail too: the passport bears a visa for the United States apparently issued by the American Embassy in Pakistan.

Shortly after Zacarias Moussaoui's arrest, on 21 August 2001, the FBI got in touch with the French secret police to gather as much information as they could about him. The American police thus learned from two memoranda dated 29 and 30 August that Zacarias Moussaoui, whose itinerary is described as 'sensitive',[2] travelled to Afghanistan in 1999, and to Pakistan. France accordingly officially alerted the United States to the fact that Zacarias Moussaoui had been an activist.

This information released by the French Secret Service was included in the investigations undertaken by FBI agents, who reckoned, during the summer of 2001, that there was an imminent danger of an attack by Islamists on the United States, and a particular risk that aeroplanes would be hijacked. One such Minneapolis-based FBI agent's report even referred to the possibility that Zacarias Moussaoui might 'fly something into the World Trade Center'.[3]

Abd Samad Moussaoui, who has no time for extremist ideologies – indeed, he campaigns against them – has lost all contact with his brother, whom he last saw in 1995.

With Zacarias Moussaoui's trial just a few months away,[4] his brother is merely keen both to shed some light for us on the many and varied reasons why a life can so radically change, and to warn against the destructive ideologies that pose a threat to the international community.

PROLOGUE

13 September 2001. A Thursday. I was on my way home. I'd finished my week's classes and tidied up the little room at the secondary school I use during the week. For the past few days I'd been working as an assistant teacher, teaching electrical engineering at the vocational secondary school in Mende, about sixty miles north of Montpellier, where I live with my wife. I was quietly driving home. It was getting on for 8 p.m.

Night was falling over the Millau plateau. As it always is when the weather's clear over these uplands, the sky was thick with twinkling stars. I had the radio on. France Info, because like everyone else I needed to know how the world was faring, more or less round the clock, since those atrocious attacks on the World Trade Center and the Pentagon. On the Larzac plateau the journalist's voice faded – in these parts the airwaves get lost in the vastness…

I made the most of the silence and let my mind wander. Then, all of a sudden, coming from who knows where, a voice intruded on the pleasantly torpid state I was in. That voice was talking about me. It uttered my name, 'Moussaoui'.

It was actually my brother's name that the voice was broadcasting for all to hear: 'Zacarias Moussaoui'. Unbelievable! That voice coming from the radio was talking about my brother! Was I dreaming? No. It was a nightmare, the start of a nightmare.

'Zacarias Moussaoui, a French citizen of Algerian origin, was arrested in the United States on 16th August. He is allegedly linked with the attacks on the World Trade Center…'

Suddenly I forgot how to think straight. My brain was a muddle. I drove, concentrating on the road ahead. My hands gripped the steering wheel. I clung to a faint hope: my Zacarias Moussaoui, my brother, is not of Algerian origin. We're French, but of Moroccan origin. The Moussaoui they were talking about had to be someone with the same name.

That had to be it. It couldn't be him. But deep down inside me something had come to a standstill, as if suspended. Unfortunately I knew that it wasn't impossible; I knew it might be my Zacarias.

'Hailing from Narbonne, in southern France, Zacarias Moussaoui was arrested in Boston, Massachusetts, while he was attending flying school...'

'Hailing from Narbonne.' Could it just be that someone with the same name as my brother *also* came from that city? I wanted to stop thinking. I just wanted to get home and be with my wife and our friends.

That was a year ago. And for the past year the media have been hounding me with endless questions. The French media, and the media from all over the world, have been talking about Zacarias Moussaoui. My brother. They've also been talking about me, Abd Samad. My heart feels like there's a weight on it. Something heavy that's hard to describe. Something powerful that I can no longer keep hidden deep down in me.

In a quite natural way, little by little, in my solitude, and without thinking about it too much, I've opted for the only possible way of getting this burden off my chest. I've decided to write. So here I am, a simple person, keen to shed some light on what I know about my brother, addressing you, my readers. Who is my brother? What's his story? How could he ever get mixed up in all that horror? Could it have been avoided? I want to try to sketch out some answers to all these questions. So I'll tell you something about our life. I'll tell you what my grandmother, my mother's mother, my aunt and my uncles have all been saying out loud about our family history. I hope I will be able to make myself understood.

1

A 'FAMILY'

My maternal grandmother's name is Amina. In Arabic, Amina means 'serene, peaceful'. Her first name suits her well. My grandmother is a character, in the fullest sense of the term. She comes from a noble lineage – from the descendants of the prophet. If you trace her genealogy, going back from one generation to the next, you end up at Moulay Idriss, the great saint descended from Prophet Muhammad. The descendants of the Prophet are the Cherif, the family of the kings of Morocco.

Amina was born in Tafilelt, in Morocco's far south, ninety years ago. Needless to say, Amina lived through the colonial period. She readily tells how, in the 1920s, Tafilelt stood up to French colonization, the Legion's bombardments and the battles between French and Moroccan troops. Colonial France occupied Tafilelt, but the region was struck by famine. So Amina's family moved, heading off to the Middle Atlas and settling in Azrou, a rugged village high up in the mountains. In winter, the lanes of Azrou are covered with snow. It was in Azrou that Amina met my grandfather. He was her second husband. My grandmother doesn't talk much about her first one, with whom she had one daughter, Rouqayyah. My grandfather was called Mekki, 'the man from Mecca'. He was a lot older than my grandmother, maybe

twenty years her senior. He was a widower. In those days
widows and widowers didn't stay widows and widowers for
long.

Mekki came from a very well-off family. He had assets – he
owned several butcher's shops in the region – but he wasn't
afraid of hard work. He was a good man, renowned round
about for his great generosity towards poor people. Lots of
them would travel many miles, on donkey or by foot, be it
sunny or snowy, across the mountains to ask him for help.
Mekki would give them meat to feed their children. He was a
practising Muslim, and it was quite normal for him to give
help to the poorest.

Mekki also liked working his land. And it was on his land
that death claimed him in 1953, in the middle of harvest time.
My grandmother was just forty, and she had five children, her
daughter from the first marriage, Rouqayyah, and four
children by my grandfather: Muhammad, the eldest of the
boys, then Omar, my mother Aïcha, and my aunt Zouhour.
She was now on her own, saddled with the task of bringing up
all five of them. Alone and, to everybody's surprise, poor,
because Mekki had not managed to put one sou aside. To
survive, the first thing Amina did was sell the remaining
butcher's shop. Then being very deft with her hands,
particularly when it came to pottery, she started making
'canouns', those terracotta braziers which all cooks used at
that time, and still do at times today. She sold them at market,
and that gradually became her sole livelihood. Amina had
become poor.

Poor but not cowed. School was not compulsory, but she
was keen for her children – and her daughters especially – to
go to school. So my mother and my aunt both went to school.
My mother, Aïcha, wasn't a born student, but she was very
fond of the company of the White Fathers, who had been in
Azrou for years. My aunt, Zouhour, on the other hand, was
brilliant.

My mother was about seven, and my aunt four, when my grandfather died. My two uncles were a little bit older. I say 'about', because birth registers in those days were not as accurate as they are today. The dates were approximate ones. It was difficult for my grandmother to bring up her children and work at the same time, in a house with no father figure. Because she was unable to feed everybody with her meagre income, a cousin offered to take Aïcha into his home and raise her. Needless to say, by way of exchange Aïcha had to help with the housework.

So my mother grew up fatherless, just like her brothers and sisters. At a very young age she could think of only one thing: leaving. Aïcha had just turned fourteen when she met my father, Omar Moussaoui. He was from Fès, some forty miles from Azrou. Fès is a large city, renowned throughout Morocco and abroad for its tiles, its mosaics, and above all for the Qarawiyyin theological university. My father was a tiler. He travelled a great deal in the region for his work, wherever there was a building site. That's how he met my mother. Aïcha wanted to get married right away, so that she could leave home. To start with, my grandmother refused. Aïcha was fourteen and, to my grandmother, she was still a little girl, but in those days, in a southern Moroccan village, marrying off daughters that young was not uncommon. Aïcha dug her heels in, and my grandmother finally agreed to the marriage – and my mother stopped going to school there and then. That, anyway, is the story as told by my grandmother and my uncles and aunt. It's not at all my mother's version. Throughout our childhood, Aïcha actually kept telling us that she had been 'forced' to marry at the age of fourteen.

As soon as she was married, my mother gave birth to two children who died very young. Then, when she was about seventeen, she had Nadia, my eldest sister. Two years later, my other sister, Jamila, was born, still in Morocco, at Bine el-Ouidane. Shortly after the birth of this second daughter, my father heard about the possibility of work in France. The year was 1965, and French recruiters were going from village to village explaining to people that France was looking for craftsmen, masons and tilers who were good with their hands and hard workers. They also added that France was a rich country where the pay was good. At that time in Morocco, my father made a good living. He even had a motorbike! But he thought that working in France would bring in more money for his family, so my mother and he decided to move to France. Once again, I know all these details through my grandmother, my aunt and my uncles. My mother never talked to us herself about her childhood except to tell us that she had learned how to sew, that she had been forced into marriage, that our father was a hard man, that her mother was mean and that she had been brought up by a cousin...

The Moussaoui family set up home in Bayonne because my father knew that he could find work in the south-west. In fact he found work straight away with a tiling and building company. He was very good at his job. He could pour a concrete screed, a hundred feet by sixty-five, by eye, and without even using a spirit level he could pick out the tiniest flaw or lump. In no time he was making good money, and he even managed to buy himself a Renault 16. I remember the car well because we had an accident: the car rolled over on its roof, and we all crawled out through the back window. I also have very clear memories of the huge colour TV set which had pride of place in the living-room.

I was born two years after my parents and my sisters arrived in France, when they were living in Hendaye, in 1967, on 1 January at half-past midnight. I'm told that the doctor came to our house in his party clothes. My brother Zacarias was born in St-Jean-de-Luz on 30 May 1968. Three years after his birth, on 28 June 1971, my parents were divorced in Bayonne. I have absolutely no memories of scenes of family violence. But I was still very young at the time. What I do remember, on the other hand, is the day when my mother told us: 'We're going to a holiday camp.' 'We' meant 'she and us', her children. So all five of us left home and went to the Dordogne. I was about four and Zacarias three. Aïcha had found a job as a laundress in that very holiday camp. She had small lodgings there. I don't remember her ever explaining to us that she had left my father. The fact was that from one day to the next we simply weren't living with him any more...

It was summer, there were bikes in the camp and we went on beautiful bike rides. For us it was like a holiday, a totally different day-to-day atmosphere because my father wasn't there. When I think about it, I don't have many memories of my father, but Zacarias can't have any at all, because he was so young when we left our father. After the Dordogne, September came and we went even further away, to Mulhouse. What a change! The only thing that didn't change was that my father was still not with us. Why Mulhouse? Because my mother had found a job there. I don't know how, and I don't know what the job was.

No sooner had we arrived in that city in Alsace than my mother put my two sisters, my brother and me in an orphanage. Because she couldn't keep us with her, the local Social Services Department took care of us in her stead. So from one day to the next we found ourselves both fatherless and motherless. I have very few memories of those grim childhood years, but they are dreadful ones. The youth workers were very kind, but all of us had the feeling that we were not like the other kids. Zacarias and I looked at them as if they were Martians! And even the youth workers seemed strange to us. We weren't too sure what they expected of us. I remember in particular one 31 December when they came and woke us up at midnight, to celebrate my fifth birthday. They had made mulled wine. Even today, I still have very clear memories of certain details in that orphanage: for example the way the rooms were furnished. I remember the wooden floors and the spiral staircases. We slept two to a room, and the beds were made of wood, with large cosy eiderdowns to keep us warm. It gets cold in the winter in Mulhouse. The boys' building was separated from the girls' by a courtyard which the refectory looked out on.

I spent all my time with my brother. Thank God they didn't separate us! Zacarias was quite small, still only three or four years old. My sisters lived in the girls' building but we would meet up during the day. In fact my big sister Nadia never let us out of her sight. Perhaps my mother had told her to keep an eye on us. It has to be said that all sorts of things went on in that orphanage. Some of the older children took drugs, and others prostituted themselves. We took great care not to be like them, not to use the vulgar language they did, and, to avoid, among the older kids, the toughest. Some of those children really were suffering from a real lack of emotional warmth.

So Zac and I were inseparable. We were always together, be it in the yard or the refectory. We played a lot of ball games, bench-ball and soccer. We also had stilts. Our best game was stilt fights!

He and I lived through those years as if they were an interlude. We didn't really understand what we were doing in the orphanage. But we had a pretty good hunch that our situation wasn't altogether normal. We were careful, though, not to think too much about it, in the hope that we wouldn't spend too long in the place. We were quite sure we wouldn't. When you're a kid, you have a special notion of time. Fortunately enough, that situation did not last for more than a year.

We knew that we were there because our mother had left our father and she didn't have enough money to take care of us. With every passing day we would say over and over that we weren't going to stay long in the orphanage, we were quite sure about that, our mother had promised us. Every day, we would nag my big sister Nadia to find out when our mother was going to come and fetch us. And every time we nagged, Nadia tirelessly and patiently answered: 'Soon…' But we got a bit worried from time to time. I don't recall my mother taking us home for weekends, or ever taking us out of the orphanage. She came to see us about once a week, but she never took us back home. Maybe she did not yet have a 'place of her own'.

One day, she really did come and get us, once and for all. Oddly enough, although I have other clear memories of that period, I have absolutely no recall of that particular day. I remember only one thing: after the orphanage, we lived on the Rue des Châtaigniers in a rather classy apartment building. There were nice carpets on the floor and a lift with big mirrors. We had a large apartment on the fourth floor. The contrast with the orphanage was striking. For Zacarias and me, our mother was a heroine, a fighter who did everything she could for her children and made sacrifices for our happiness. Hadn't she just rescued us from the orphanage?

Aïcha then found a job as a cleaning woman in the central post office in Mulhouse. The inspector in her department was called Joseph Klifa. Later on he became mayor of the city and was famous for belonging to the Republican Alliance against the extreme right in the region. Joseph Klifa felt sorry for my mother and her precarious situation – a woman on her own with four children touched him. She would actually tell anyone who wanted to hear it that she had been forced into marriage in Morocco. One fine day, after she had obtained French nationality, Joseph Klifa helped her to get a permanent position, she became a post office employee.

She worked early in the morning and late at night, once the post office had closed. As the eldest child, my sister Nadia, now aged twelve, took over my mother's role at home. She did the shopping and the cooking and the housework and looked after us. At night she would make us supper and in the morning she would help us to get dressed. And there was no messing about or else the slaps fell thick and fast! My other sister, Jamila, backed her up. And it took two of them to keep an eye on Zacarias and me!

Once again the family moved house, this time to an apartment on the Bourtzwiller estate. Bourtzwiller was what is now commonly known as 'a problem neighbourhood'. At that time Zacarias and I thought only about having fun. We went to school to have fun, and we came out of school and had more fun. Fun was our only and constant concern. Boys will be boys...

At our school there was a notorious family by the name of Deau[1] with seventeen children. It was better not to get on their wrong side, because there was strength in their sheer numbers. If you got into an argument with one of them, the other sixteen might come to his aid, and that was awful. For example, Zacarias had fights with a Deau boy of his own age and in no time things escalated: the Deau boy called his big brother and Zacarias called me. But the second Deau son called his even bigger brother, so I had to call for help from my sister Jamila. She was awesome when it came to defending us. She could pack a punch as well as any boy. And if that didn't do the trick, if the Deau boy got just a little bit too big for his boots, we would call Nadia. Unfortunately, Nadia was our last trump card, and they still had at least thirteen more to come...

At school, we also got up to a lot of high jinks. One September, all the kids in the neighbourhood agreed that term was starting too early. So we all thought about the best way of squeezing out a few more days from the holiday, and we found it! A day or two before we were due back at school, in mid-afternoon, some of the kids got into the school. They took all the chairs and tables into a classroom and then painstakingly spray-painted them. The beginning of term was delayed for a week. For us it was a victory!

Zac and I liked to organize bike races, but because our

bikes were too big (they were salvaged jobs with a bar in the middle) we had to lean left and then right to reach the pedals. It really hurt when you missed a pedal! We were really reckless. Our favourite game involved climbing up the drainpipes to the roof as quickly as we could. We organized speed competitions with the other boys to prove our bravery and agility.

At that time on our housing estate many of us came from North Africa. We all got on well together, except with families renowned for their dislike of foreigners. In our building lived the Kol family and the parents were very racist. And when Alsatians are racist, it's quite something! When the Kols bumped into Zac and me, they called us 'dirty niggers'. Not 'dirty Arabs', but 'dirty niggers'. Probably because my brother and I are quite dark-skinned. They didn't make any distinction between Arabs and blacks; we were quite simply just not whites. One day, for no particular reason, their eldest son, who must have been fifteen or sixteen, insulted us, and that set off a general brawl. He was really mean and quite a lot bigger than us. In the free-for-all, he threw me against an iron post which got stuck in my back. I ended up in hospital, and I've still got a scar.

Near the Bourtzwiller estate there were some ponds. We built rafts and had sea battles. For us, in those years real life happened outdoors. As soon as we could, Zac and I slipped out of the house. In the apartment, life wasn't up to much. My mother didn't have much time for us; she always had other things to do. It would have been misguided to expect the slightest tender word from her or the merest gesture of affection. She didn't know how to do that. As for my sisters, who nevertheless did more than just back her up, my mother often scolded them too. So Zac and I kept ourselves to ourselves, giving each other support. At school we did nothing, or next to nothing. But in spite of that, my brother and I always just managed to go up into the next class, simply because we weren't stupid. It was in my fifth year of primary school, when I was ten or eleven, that I realized that it was better to work a little bit, and, at the same time, Zacarias realized that too.

When we were living in Bourtzwiller, our father came to see us now and then – or rather, he *tried* to see us. For us this was still some kind of a game, and this game had very strict rules laid down by my mother. She had trained us. She told us that our father had hurt her, that he was a hard man and that she would be greatly upset if we agreed to see him. My father would come and we would run off, just as she had told us to do. All four of us, all in different directions. We were running away from the big bad wolf. Poor man!

I remember one of those episodes particularly well. My father had given us advance notice that he was coming because he had visiting rights. My mother told us: 'OK, he'll be here about 2 p.m., so just before that, you all disappear.' We obeyed her. When my father arrived and realized that we weren't in the apartment, instead of wasting time arguing with my mother, he started looking for us everywhere in the neighbourhood. He had travelled miles to see us. We were young and he was pretty sure that we hadn't gone far away. Maybe he didn't even know that we were hiding. Maybe he thought that my mother hadn't told us he was coming. When he finally found us, he said: 'Come on, let's have a walk together!' And we ran away again, just like that. All of a sudden he ran after us, caught us and put us in his car. As soon as he'd started the engine, Zac and I exchanged a single glance, there being no need for words in so perilous a situation. At the same time, we opened the car doors and leaped out of the car. If we hadn't done that, we would no longer have been our mother's sons!...

This scene was repeated many times, until my father finally gave up, I think, when he understood that my mother had turned us against him. And he must have told himself that when we became old enough, we would decide for ourselves if we wanted to see him. From that moment on, our mother sang a different tune, telling us constantly: 'Well! See how your father's abandoned you!'

Not long after that, my mother met another man, Saïd, who moved in with us. My mother worked, received family allowances and was extremely thrifty. She ended up managing to buy a small house – one of those detached ones built for workers in the old potash mines in the very heart of Mulhouse. I clearly remember the price, at the time – 120,000 francs – it was all my mother talked about. That house had a ground floor, two upper floors and a large garden. We made some alterations on one of the upper floors. There was a shed in the garden which we did up. It was at number 8, Rue du Kaysersberg, in the centre near the Boulevard Stoessel.

Saïd was like a stepfather to us. At least he was the guy who stayed longest. He was quite OK and he didn't bother us. Come what may, it was my mother who wore the trousers, and it was 'her' very own house, as she never failed to remind him, incidentally. He never answered back, never. He worked at Peugeot, and when he wasn't at the factory he tended his vegetable allotment which he had rented; we went there every weekend. This was his great love, growing fruit and vegetables on his patch of land. He came originally from the Rif Mountains, in northern Morocco – a region of people who own land. He was fond of working the land, growing beans, strawberries and tomatoes. I think my mother and he must have sold some of the produce, because our daily fare tended to be buttered slices of bread and white coffee. Throughout her life, my mother never stopped saying how she had to keep making savings.

One day Saïd wanted to take me to work with him on the allotment. Because I didn't feel like going, he forced me to sit on his knees in the front of the Peugeot 204. He somehow managed to drive with me wriggling around on his knees, but once we got to the end of the street, I bit him, which meant he couldn't turn the wheel, and the car went straight into a tree. The 204 was a write-off.

Near the housing estate were slag heaps which local people called Mount Coqrourie. They were large mounds with a wood and a little river. We heard tales about these places which alarmed and intrigued us. So our great challenge was to go and walk among them to scare ourselves. You had to show how brave you were to cross the Coqrourie without being caught. We would go there shaking with fear and the slightest noise would make us run off as fast as our legs could carry us, shouting: 'They're there! They're there!' And all the neighbourhood kids scrammed, like rabbits.

In those days we had roller skates and skateboards. We also collected racing bikes, which were too big for us, and which we took wherever we found them. We would throw them into the canal, right close to the edge. Then we would go home and that evening we would ask our stepfather to walk with us beside the canal. When we got near the canal, my brother and I would exclaim: 'Oh! A bike in the canal!' Our stepfather would help us drag it from the water, happy at our godsend. So we had at least a dozen bikes at home. Every time we went off for a walk, we would 'find' a bike. One day my stepfather must have caught on, because after dragging a bicycle out of the water he said to Zacarias, who had thoughts about taking it for himself: 'But that's my bike, I'm the one who got it out!' Zacarias was dumbfounded; he hadn't expected any such reaction.

Another time, when I was coming out of school, I didn't feel like walking home and I spied a small bike. Without a moment's hesitation, I took it, went home on it and chucked it into the canal as usual. But this time, somebody saw me, and the owner turned up at home, found Nadia and Zacarias, and said to them: 'Someone saw your brother take the bike. He'd better give it back, right away.' When I got home, and my brother asked me about it, I said: 'It's not true, it wasn't me!' Needless to say, he believed me. He was furious. He went to see the owner of the bike and said to him: 'How can you accuse my brother of being a thief? He didn't steal it. If he did, I'd know about it! You can't accuse someone without any proof, that's a false accusation, and it's serious for my brother's reputation in the neighbourhood...' Incredible reasoning coming from the mouth of an eight-year-old kid. There was my little brother lecturing a grown-up to get me off the hook. And it was because that injustice had shocked him. Suddenly the guy started to have doubts, and he dropped the whole thing. Later, I told Zacarias the truth and he balled me out.

But the favourite 'sport' of the neighbourhood kids was to attack buses with slingshots. One day the driver we attacked spun his bus right around, chased after us, and once he'd caught up with us leaped out of the bus like a madman and grabbed me by the neck. I was scared stiff, but because I'd already got rid of the slingshot, I yelled out: 'It wasn't me! It wasn't me!' Once again, my brother came to my rescue and told the driver: 'It wasn't him. It's a serious matter to accuse people without proof!' But this time around the guy wasn't having any of that. He took my brother and me back home and my mother reprimanded us in front of him. And then, as soon as his back was turned, she hissed: 'We don't give a damn about that guy. Get out of here!'

When we lived on the Bourtzwiller estate, my sister Nadia was at secondary school. She looked after the house, and us, and what's more she was very clever. The headmaster said she was his best student. Nadia had black, frizzy hair. She was tall. A pretty girl, she danced and acted. Later on, in Mulhouse, we all went to see her perform in her first play. Jamila was something different, though. As long as my brother and I were small, there was an alliance between our sisters: the two big

kids against the two little ones. And then one day all that
changed. The day when they realized that I was as strong as
they were, and possibly even stronger. It was from that
moment on that Jamila turned into a punchbag. Who got
scolded when one of us did something silly? Jamila. Who got
slapped? Jamila. Zacarias and I felt for her.

She had become a scapegoat, and we tried to defend her.
Zacarias especially. He was very kind to Jamila and very fond
of her. It was when we went to live in Rue du Kaysersberg
that the situation between Jamila and my mother became
really poisoned. It all started with a croissant. Every morning
my mother bought a croissant at the bakery as she went off to
work. The croissant cost two francs, and every night my
mother put a two-franc coin in her wallet for the next day. But
one morning, the coin wasn't there. Someone had taken it.
She didn't bother to find out who, and immediately laid into
Jamila. My mother was furious. And Jamila hadn't even taken
it.

Divide and rule was my mother's strategy. But it didn't
work at all with my brother and me. We were so close to one
another that she came up against an insurmountable wall
when she tried to favour one over the other. She found it
easier to divide her daughters. She had a real technique. She
would take one of them to one side and say: 'You're the more
beautiful. You're my favourite.' Then she would say the same
thing to the other daughter, thus pitting one against the other.
And then, to punish us, my mother would often use a strap.

Zacarias was an ideal younger brother. He was smart,
clever and kind. He was a really nice boy. The nicest of our
group, I think. He and I were really close, and we really liked
one another a lot. I think that we just knew, without ever
saying as much out loud, that in this life we could only really
count on each other. We tried to avoid getting mixed up in
family feuds. We suspected them to be a source of problems,
screams and blows. We were often quite naughty, but never in

a mean or violent way – the naughty things kids do, to have a laugh, not to do any harm.

In 1974 we discovered Morocco, our country of origin, for the first time. What a trip! I have wonderful memories of it. We set off by train. It was an expedition no less. A mother with her four children in a train! I remember it was very hot, and there were water vendors in the Spanish stations. Here, again, Nadia organized everything down to the last detail. I was seven and Zacarias five and a half. I remember my aunt's cakes, huge watermelons and prickly pear fruit. The weather was very fine, and we played in the streets with our cousins. Pure bliss, an outstanding summer. We went back by car with our stepfather in the summer of 1977. I was ten. It's a long way from Mulhouse to Taourirt. Zacarias and I slipped into the back of the 204 station wagon among the luggage to get some sleep.

Once in Morocco, the sort of things my mother said changed completely. She who usually grumbled about working herself to death and how hard life was would tell the whole Moroccan family that we had a very comfortable life in France; that money grew on trees there, and that all you needed to succeed was a desire to succeed. I have moving memories of the Morocco of our childhood. For my mother and me, that is where our family is.

Throughout our stays there, our grandmother and our aunt attended to our every need. They didn't see much of us and as soon as we arrived they would start spoiling us, Zacarias particularly, probably because he was the youngest. They gave us pastries which they made themselves, *makrouds*, honey and almond cakes, and *zlabias*, colourful, translucent sweets made of pure sugar. Sometimes, too, when my mother wasn't looking, they would give us a little pocket money, and we would slip away and buy sweets at the corner shop. There were always lots of us at mealtimes, and a tajine or two were always simmering on the fire. And then, for us, Morocco meant meeting up again with our cousins, boys and girls. We found everything new and interesting.

On Sundays, we went with our cousins to the Koranic school. But Zacarias and I hardly knew what the Koran was, so the Koranic school... But we liked it well enough and found it very unusual at the same time: all those children in a large room, repeating after the teacher the verses of that holy book, which neither our mother nor stepfather ever talked to us about... There were children of all ages there, the smallest at the front, the biggest at the back, and the teacher used reeds of different lengths to reach each head. That's where we first heard the chant: '*Bismillah r-Rahmani r-Rahim...*' (In the name of God the lenient, the merciful), which we memorized very quickly, enough at least to repeat it with great vigour. Those were very lovely holidays.

Usually we spent all our school holidays and Wednesdays at a drop-in centre. One day Zacarias and I had had enough of it, and we badgered our mother to sign us up for sports activities on Wednesdays. First we did judo and karate, then Zacarias played handball and I played basketball.

For Zacarias, handball quickly became more than a sport – it was his passion. He played at the Mulhouse Sports Club. He was brilliant. One of his old handball pals, Thomas, who subsequently played in the first division, remembers Zacarias very well, particularly because he had a particular mannerism: when he played he would stick out the tip of his tongue and bite it as he hit the ball. Everybody was afraid that a bad shot would cut his tongue off! Zacarias's gifts were unanimously recognized by his trainers, his teammates, and even his opponents. He had a difficult position, playing guard like Jackson Richardson in the French team! Zacarias played in various championships and his team won first the district championships, and then the Alsace championships. I loved going to watch him play and support him. For Zacarias, the future was all mapped out. He would study and play sports.

Things between our mother and Jamila got worse and worse. They started out stormy and became explosive. Jamila started to run away from home, and every time it was up to Zacarias and me to find her. As soon as they bumped into each other in the house, they started quarrelling. Aïcha had taken a sudden dislike to her daughter, and yet, God knows, Jamila did everything she could to see her mother as little as possible. One Sunday my mother came into my bedroom to talk to me the way she did whenever she wanted me to help her sort out a problem. 'OK, I'd like you to do me a favour. I'm going to send your sister away to school, because this just isn't working. She's rude and bad-mannered, and she doesn't do a thing at school. I can't cope with her any more. Boarding school will be good for her. Do you want to go too? That way she won't be all alone?' It seemed a good idea to me. Sending Jamila away could only make things better between them.

My mother had her reasons to get my advice. She knew I was attached to Zacarias and Jamila and she felt that I had compassion for my sister. And then the choice was quickly made: there was no question of her being separated from Nadia, whom she loved and who was very useful for her. As for Zacarias, he was too young to be a boarder. Her calculations were on the nail. I didn't have the heart to let my sister go off alone to boarding school, so I agreed to my mother's proposal. Zacarias was sad when I left, because for him it was a bit like I was abandoning him. But he too didn't want his favourite sister to end up alone at a boarding school. He was forced to admit that I really didn't have any other choice.

So my sister and I went to school the following term in Altkirch, a little village twelve miles from Mulhouse in the depths of Alsace. I was in the sixth class, as a first-year pupil, and she was in the fourth. The year started out hard – I missed Zacarias and he missed me. He was bored without his brother and found himself even more exposed to family rows.

He was champing at the bit, all on his own. Luckily for him, he had handball.

So we spent all week as boarders. For Jamila and me it wasn't unpleasant. It was something of an adventure, our apprenticeship in freedom. That was the year I smoked my first cigarettes. It was also a year when my mother could have a bit of a rest – now just two children at home, my sister Nadia, better than housemaid, because she wasn't paid anything, and my brother Zacarias, who was still a boy. Jamila and I went home every weekend.

Zacarias and I hugged each other every time we were back together. We made sure we spent all weekend with each other. That's also why I was such a keen and privileged supporter at his handball matches.

As the year slowly passed, I realized that daily life was really not a bed of roses for my little brother. Invariably out of some sort of shame, Zacarias actually only rarely told me the details about his rows with my mother, but all the same he did confess to me that now that I was no longer at home he was always on the alert, ready to dodge his mother's fits of anger. But no matter how hard he tried, he didn't always manage to.

Towards the end of the year, my mother gathered us all together one weekend to tell us that she wanted to apply for a job transfer at the post office. What she had in mind was 'to go somewhere sunny'. One of us immediately answered negatively: Zacarias. 'I won't go. Next year I want to study sports at Mulhouse,' he explained to us. My mother pretended not to have heard him and got out a map of France to show us several cities where her seniority would allow her to be transferred to: Montpellier, Narbonne, Perpignan and Béziers. We took a ruler to measure on the map which city was closest to the sea, and Narbonne was the winner. My mother decided to get us to vote on it, and Zacarias was the only one against moving house. Together with my sisters, I imagined the sea, the sun and holidays all year round. We didn't care a bit about leaving Mulhouse; Zacarias was the only one who was attached to that city. With hindsight, I think that after the ordeal of the orphanage, that move to Narbonne was another great wrench for him. It meant the end of his dream of becoming a professional handball player and then perhaps a coach...

2

TEENAGE YEARS: FUN TIMES AND FRUSTRATIONS

When we moved, I was thirteen and Zacarias was twelve. For weeks before we finally left Mulhouse, throughout all our packing up, he would grumble: 'I don't want to go there! Narbonne's a dump! Anyway, I'm not going! I want to stay in Mulhouse.' Needless to say, he had to come with us. We were still children, and our major preoccupation was having a good time and getting up to no good together. But in spite of everything, from that moment on, something in Zacarias changed. There was a sort of uncertainty about him, a slight shift, an edge of bitterness and rancour. Like a very fine scar, hardly visible, which time never heals. Zacarias would always miss Mulhouse or, rather, the life he imagined he'd have had there – the life of a handball champion. When we left Mulhouse our living conditions changed overnight. In Alsace, we lived in a large house with a big garden and a shed. We all had our own rooms. In Narbonne, where we moved in late August, we rediscovered the 'charms' of the housing estate, the real thing, just like in TV reports: the Razimbaud estate, fourth floor. The first time we walked into the apartment we were a bit shocked by the bathroom where a hip-bath had pride of place – we'd never seen anything quite so ridiculous. There were just two rooms for the children: one for the boys, the other for the girls.

When we arrived we didn't know anybody in the neighbourhood. We were happy just to look around, until it was time to start school a few weeks later. When our mother had the time, she took us to the sea. We started at the Montesquieu secondary school, which was close to where we lived. It was a difficult moment because we were complete strangers in the school, and Zacarias was starting in year six. He was still much more apprehensive than I was about discovering a totally new, and possibly hostile, environment. All the more so because we had a major disadvantage: our Alsatian accent. It was impossible to go unnoticed with an accent like that, especially in French lessons. What's more, we were the only 'Blacks' in Narbonne who spoke with an Alsatian accent. The contrast, needless to say, made everybody laugh. Except us. Shopkeepers, student supervisors, some of the teachers, but above all our classmates and our neighbours all looked at us in an odd way.

If I use the term 'Blacks' to describe us, even though we are Arabs, it's because the dark colour of our skin causes a particular reaction among born-and-bred French people – an inability to stick an exact label on us at first glance. They are often hesitant about our origins – the only thing they're certain of is that we come from somewhere else. From Africa, or from the Caribbean? To find out they have no option but to ask us, and it's only when we answer that we are 'North Africans', or 'Moroccans', that they understand that we are Arabs. I've lived with this ambiguity throughout my life, and so has Zacarias. Now that I'm an adult, and settled, it no longer bothers me – I've got used to it. But as children, Zacarias and I found it extremely unpleasant to be so often forced to explain our origins because of the colour of our skin. Repeating it had something humiliating and unsettling about it, because it meant that we weren't *identifiable* at first sight. As if we didn't have any formal identity. And what's even more humiliating is the negative, furtive but spontaneous reaction from those for whom people from the Caribbean are French 'in spite of everything', whereas Arabs...

It was a slow process getting acclimatized to the housing estate and school. Below our building there was a handball court, and Zacarias made a beeline for it. But the neighbourhood kids had their habits and they weren't prepared to welcome a newcomer just like that – even less such a good player. I followed Zac on to the court and needless to say we won more or less every game. But we didn't necessarily win the fights which started up at the same time. Here too there were large families, of course, but Zacarias and I were older, and calling our sisters to our defence was out of the question. The brawls were more violent than they had been in Alsace.

It took us a good two years before we felt 'at home' in the south. On the Razimbaud estate the boys who were older than us were really tough. Each building had its gang and its gang leader. For months on end, it was impossible for us to become part of one of the gangs. Without a gang, it was very hard to be accepted in the neighbourhood. A few weeks before we'd arrived in Narbonne, a dozen or so young guys from the estate, aged between fifteen and twenty-three, raped a young woman on the beach after beating up her husband. A few of them were arrested and put in jail; others fled the country. Several families on the Razimbaud estate were strongly implicated, to a greater or lesser degree, in this ugly incident. So at the time that we arrived there, the housing estate was still abuzz with this painful affair, and the overall climate was heavy.

Families from all over North Africa and native French families lived in our building. At that time the Razimbaud estate had a number-one enemy: the neighbouring estate, where pretty much only people of French origin lived, which was called the Pastouret. Obviously, the Pastouret became the fascist estate, and Razimbaud the estate of Arabs and French – the melting-pot estate. Another estate, St-Jean-St-Pierre, one of those estates forgotten by liberals who sleep well at night, was more or less exclusively lived in by North Africans and Turks. Depending on the day and the mood, this estate would either support or attack us. One thing was for sure, however: whatever disagreements there might have been between Razimbaud and St-Jean-St-Pierre, the two neighbourhoods were united against the Pastouret, the fascists' estate. The honour of the Arabs (and in this specific instance 'Arabs' is used as a generic term to describe all the inhabitants of a neighbourhood) was safe and sound.

At the ages of thirteen and fourteen respectively, Zacarias and I were none the less content to stand on the sidelines and observe. We didn't take part in the really serious fights. Except for one unforgettable time. There was a big party at Razimbaud and the kids from St-Jean-St-Pierre, who hadn't been invited, wanted in. The whole scene quickly degenerated into an orderly battle, right in the middle of the street. Thirty young people mixing it. Zac and I managed to get into the thick of it without taking any nasty knocks. We were hidden behind two huge bruisers from our estate, and as soon as they pinned an enemy to the ground we'd leap on him, while the two guys, who were built like tanks, went about the business of bringing in the next customer.

In that kind of neighbourhood, there was just one simple rule: unless the others feared you, you were nothing. So the aim was to make people afraid of you as a matter of practice. And things happened fast. After two years, Zacarias and I also knew how to make people respect us. We were a bunch of about fifteen kids whose families had moved into the apartment block at the same time, and we formed our own gang. Among the newcomers, one family came from northern France, with two burly sons who, like us, had an accent you could cut with a knife.

Our friend Jacques lived just below us. His family was very hospitable and we made the most of it. His mother was a politically committed woman, a trade unionist. We could talk for hours on end with her about politics, society and the future... Jacques' father was a sales rep for a brand of coffee. In their house there was always room at the table, and coffee was always brewing. Whenever we could – several times a day – Zac and I went downstairs to see them. Sometimes we went back home only to sleep, when we didn't sleep-over. For us, that family was a real family, warm and noisy, not noisy with shouting, rather with laughter. During the 1982 World Cup, we more or less moved in with them. That was a real party. Jacques' family had a soft spot for Zacarias in particular. For them he was the estate's mascot. I should add that Zac could really lay on the charm; his kindness, subtlety, thoughtfulness and wit won many a heart. And above all he liked helping people he appreciated.

In our apartment block there was also a 'bike specialist' called Jean. He would steal bicycle and motorcycle parts and use them to assemble his own machines. That's how we got to know him – he had walked off with the derailler on my bike. Because I had put my own mark on it, I recognized it at once outside his garage. So I went to see Jean and, with Zacarias with me, ordered him to give me back my derailler, telling him how I knew it was mine. He was a good sport, so he agreed to let me have it back, and that's how we became friends. Jean had a brother and two half-brothers, really big guys who were a bit our 'comprehensive insurance policy' in the neighbourhood. Jean and his brothers secretly used several empty cellars in our building where they piled up their collection of bikes and spare parts. They had the very latest deraillers there, as well as revolutionary pumps and the mudguards of the future... Sometimes Zacarias and I would join them on their Saturday afternoon bike rides. We would return home exhausted, after covering a hundred miles. We were unable to walk for two days afterwards, but they were back on the road the very next day.

The bike thieves introduced us to other thieves, one of them being David, the estate's daredevil, who was my age. He was an orphan; his parents had died in a car crash. His grandmother did her level best to bring him up, for better or for worse. His uncle, a petty thief, was at that time in Carcassonne jail and something of a hero to his nephew. With a family like that, David didn't go unnoticed in the neighbourhood. He spent most of his time breaking into telephone kiosks, or stealing bikes and motorbikes and cars... anything he could get his hands on. He also launched the stock-car craze but with other people's cars. At the age of fourteen, he was stealing top-of-the-range Citroëns as well as 2 CVs. One day he lost the cops on the estate: he knew every nook and cranny there. David was definitely something of a neighbourhood hero.

We kept our distance from all those thieves, and thus from David, possibly because of our old orphanage memories and our mistrust, in those days, of badly brought-up kids, or rather kids who weren't brought up at all; future delinquents. It was David who told us you could go to jail for thieving from the age of thirteen onwards. That was a warning for us, even if the threat didn't curtail his activities. I should mention that neither Zacarias nor I looked like hoodlums. If anything, we were scared stiff of not being able to study because of having a criminal record. If there was one thing we were really sure about, it was that we wanted to go to university.

Zacarias, in particular, was obsessed by the fear of the delinquency that was potentially lying in wait for us, the way it poses a threat to all young people on housing estates living in difficult conditions, and he was afraid for me too. He warned me about spending time in the 'bad company' of those gangs of fifteen or twenty young guys, and he advised me to be careful not to get mixed up in any dodgy business.

We did pretty well at school without much effort. But as Zac and I enjoyed more or less total freedom at home, in class we weren't exactly model students. That particular year, I totted up about sixty hours of detention, and they asked us to

find another school because of our lack of discipline. So we
ended up at the Jules-Ferry secondary school on the other side
of town. It could take us up to forty-five minutes to get there
on foot. It was a totally different environment from Montesquieu. It was much more upper crust. Jules-Ferry had a
reputation for being 'the school for middle-class kids'. All of a
sudden our daily lives had changed. The school was located in
the midst of large, green expanses, with beautiful, well-
maintained buildings. But the day-to-day reality was none the
less not quite what it seemed. Weapons were doing the rounds
in that school – knives, coshes, even, on one occasion, a
revolver. There were lots of fights. I moved up into the third
year, but my marks were average, and not nearly as good as
they had been in my second year. And I was still just as
undisciplined. The maths teacher took a sudden dislike to me.
Zacarias, who was still in the second year, was craftier than I:
he realized that it paid to keep a low profile.

One afternoon I sprained my thumb playing handball in the
yard. It hurt and I wanted to go home. Because the supervisor
refused, I made as if to force my way past him. A school
counsellor who happened to be there tried to hold me back by
pulling on my sprained thumb. A sharp pain shot up my arm
and as a reflex I pushed him hard and, unfortunately, he fell to
the ground. The counsellor was beside himself and told me to
get in his car, saying: 'We're going to go and see your father!'

That same year, my father had in fact set up home in
Narbonne. For him, things were much better, because we no
longer ran away as soon as we saw him. He had a small
company and worked on building sites. He lived in a shabby
two-room apartment but drove about in a Mercedes 230.

The school counsellor made me get into his car and we
found my father at the building site. Needless to say, I wasn't
very proud of myself, even if I reckoned I was in the right.
When we got there, my father was in the middle of replastering
the front of a three-storey building; he was perched up a ladder

with two bags of cement propped on his left shoulder. The counsellor stopped the car for a few seconds. He looked at my father on the ladder with his bags of cement, changed his mind, and exclaimed: 'We're going back to school!' When we got back, he dismissed me, saying: 'It's OK, you can go back to class.' That left me flabbergasted. A faint smile played around his mouth. I should have suspected that he had something in mind. But at that moment I was just taken aback.

I only realized later what his plan was. Too late. At the end of the school year, the counsellor put together a vocational file for me. Instead of moving up into the fourth year, I ended up in a vocational training school. I took that as an act of personal vengeance, and all the more so because nobody had warned me: I only realized what was happening when the summer holidays were over. When the day came to go back to school, I turned up as usual at Jules-Ferry, but a supervisor turned me away, telling me that I was no longer enrolled at the school and that I was now enrolled at the Jean-Moulin vocational college, in plumbing. After two weeks in my new school, I realized that I'd been had, and that I was careering along at high speed in the slow lane.

As for Zacarias, he was in third year. But he was furious about that scheming school counsellor. We thoroughly agreed that there was a three-way racism within the state education system: one racism had to do with the colour of your skin, another was linked to your cultural origins, and the third was to do with social class. Zacarias was deeply schocked by the career path that had been foisted on me, possibly even more disgusted than I was. From that moment on, he learned to be suspicious of everybody in the state education system. His brother's trust had been betrayed, so he decided not to put any trust in the system. So as not to give the system the slightest chance of messing him about, he started to work hard, and behave himself.

In our neighbourhood, there was a mini-market where one

or two young guys would regularly wedge one of the windows so that it would stay open and they could pay a little night-time visit to the chocolate shelf. This way, they filled one of the cellars under their building with sweets. One day I found myself looking at a mound of Mars bars, Kit-Kats, Bounty bars and the like... This plunder had been put on one side for house parties. During the school holidays we would spend whole days 'defending the walls of the neighbourhood' and hanging out in stairways. Some guys drank beer; others smoked joints. For Zacarias and me, this wasn't really our thing. He didn't even smoke cigarettes. I had the odd puff, but only to be like my mates.

At secondary school, Zacarias completely gave up handball. He enrolled in a club when we arrived in Narbonne, but came back from the first training session saying that the level was low and that he wasn't going to waste his time with those people. The coach even came to our home to try to change his mind. But he was wasting his time, because when my brother makes up his mind... He was very ambitious, very demanding and extreme. At the age of fourteen he reckoned that Narbonne wouldn't provide him with the future he had been hoping for in Mulhouse in sports studies. He said that the Narbonne club wasn't up to the mark – in other words, up to *his* mark – so it was a waste of time and energy to go on training. With my brother, it's always all or nothing. When he believes in something, he does everything in his powers to reach his goal. But if he's disappointed, it's all over, and he draws the line from one day to the next.

Later on he tried vaguely to get involved in rugby by joining the Narbonne Racing Club, then French champions. He wasn't bad, and played on the wing. He trained for two seasons and then complained about some coaches being racists. My brother said that, at rugby, even if Arabs were good, they weren't selected for the team. At that time, according to Zacarias, the rugby world in Narbonne was full of fascists. He explained to me that for the rugby players he hung out with, a 'good Arab' was one they would go on a pub-crawl with and then smash his face in at the end of the booze-up...

A year went by in that new school. Zacarias was fifteen, and he'd made some good friends. The third-year class marked another turning point for him because he switched social circles, at least as far as the people he hung out with were concerned. At Jules-Ferry, he met the children of middle-class people, managers and teachers, who brought up their children with the future all mapped out and heading towards university. These children were also taken for holidays to the four corners of the earth. It was another life. Unlike ours, that particular world was open to what was going on outside it, and it brought us new vistas. Did Zacarias suffer by living among them without being like them? Doubtless he did, but in silence. In any event, it was during those years that he forged his closest friendships: Yves, whose father owned a business which he would naturally take over, and Maurice, whose father was a property developer.

Until he started to go off the rails, Zacarias stayed very close to his friends. What's more, the last person in his group to see him in France would be Yves, with whom he drank a few beers when he passed through in 1997. Yves had set up a billiard room and a disco in his basement and Zacarias very often hung out there. From time to time my brother's mates invited me to their homes. One of them, whose father owned a plumbing company, had an indoor swimming pool in his house. It was by spending time with those particular people, at that particular time, that my brother realized what the power of money represents. It was a turning point for him. He was very attached to his friends and his friends returned his friendship. They played rugby and went out together.

However, at the end of his fourth year I was surprised by his behaviour. He requested a move to a vocational school to do the Certificate of Technical Education as a mechanic and fitter. Was he suffering from an inferiority complex, or was he trying to take the same path that I had? At first I was puzzled, but I finally realized that he quite simply lacked self-confidence and felt humiliated because of his social roots. The son of a Moroccan cleaning woman in the midst of sons of company directors? La Croix secondary school, where he could have done his fifth year, had a reputation in our neighbourhood for being very middle class, and amongst its pupils were reputed to be some little fascists. I don't know if this was true, but for my brother, 'very middle class' meant 'very different from him', in any event. This was school where you had to wear the latest fashion, sport Nikes and have a brand new backpack. Not possible. Zacarias finally explained his choice to me with a few pithy words: 'I was all on my own.' On his own socially? All his friends were certainly moving up into the fifth year at La Croix, but who among them was able to share his unrest? If I had been at La Croix, he would probably have reacted differently, because when the hard knocks came there would have been the two of us.

In spite of everything, I tried to make him change his mind. I explained to him that the vocational school was the very opposite of the fast track, and that he was the only one of us who could succeed with flying colours. Even if it was hard at the outset, he would have to grit his teeth, knock a few heads together, and everything would be fine. But was I persuasive enough? Deep down, I understood him so well, my young brother, and I knew perfectly well that he was right, that he would never really feel like the others because he wasn't like them. Our mother wasn't much help to him. She would repeat to him, as she would to me: 'Choose what you want, I trust you. In any event, don't dream. I don't have the money to pay for your studies. You'll have to work.'

Unwittingly, I probably influenced Zacarias's drift towards a technical training certificate. Aware of having been steered towards what some regarded as a dead end, where people accepted what was in store for them because their heart wasn't in it, I myself started to study very seriously, first to get my vocational diploma and then to go for my advanced vocational diploma. And I realized that, at the end of the day, working in a workshop, where you learn practical things, and how to work copper, steel and lead, gave me a lot of satisfaction. I came into contact with enthusiastic teams of teachers, who managed to encourage in me a liking for a job well done. As a result, when I discussed day-to-day life at the vocational school with Zacarias, I projected an image of fulfilment, and for him it was a much more appealing option than an unrealistic baccalauréat[1] in a middle-class secondary school and then even more unrealistic university.

So he switched schools and joined me at the vocational college. In no time he realized he'd made a mistake: for the Certificate of Technical Education, the level was low, and he realized that the students weren't there because they wanted to be, but because they had no choice. They had been labelled 'bad', so the state educational system had pushed them down that dead-end track. Zacarias couldn't stand it. His pride took a dive.

As the years passed, my sister Nadia grew further and further away from the family, the flipside perhaps of her devotion to us when we were very small. For our mother, her eldest daughter was an artist, she did the general baccalauréat and got excellent grades, but, encouraged by our mother, she stopped her studies and enrolled at the Perpignan Drama School. For Aïcha was convinced that her daughter would become a star. And my mother, who nevertheless knew what things cost, even rented a small apartment for her.

The teachers and the headmaster at the school tried to convince my mother and my sister that they were making a big mistake. They even came to our home to talk about it. But nothing could change my mother's mind. She would say to anybody who would listen that her daughter was an artist, a future star, and that her name would be up there in lights. Our name would indeed become famous, much later on – alas…

Nadia came home only from time to time. This gave her an even more favoured status – that of the prodigal child. Imagine what it was like for my mother to see her daughter on the road to fame and fortune. Nadia wasn't a bad actress, and she went off to Paris to another drame school.

Wisely, Zacarias and I rarely got involved in these family ups and downs. Of course, we lived in the same apartment as my mother, our stepfather and our sisters. Mornings, we would see them at breakfast; evenings, at supper; and sometimes when we got back from school before we met up with our group of friends. But we didn't feel that we belonged to a family. The idea of 'home' was very vague for us. We lived under the same roof, we depended on our mother for food, but we stubbornly refused to depend on her for anything else – especially affection. For us, that would have been betting away our wellbeing and good spirits. Whenever possible, to avoid arguments, we even shunned any kind of discussion with her.

My mother's character was very changeable. She lost her temper easily and sometimes turned violent. So it was better to give her the least possible pretext. My sister Jamila ended up showing signs of depression. She who had once been a very pretty girl, small and delicate, started to put on weight. At meals, my mother would bombard her with criticism. Regularly, in the middle of eating she would endlessly reproach her, sometimes even in the presence of strangers. Depending on her mood, my sister would either ignore her or answer her back; when she did answer back, it ended in shouts and sobs.

Little by little, Jamila's behaviour become weirder and weirder. At night, she would sometimes wander about outside, and she was assaulted more than once. She ended up going to see a social worker to try to get a place in a hostel. My mother met the social worker. She told us she had explained to the social worker that her daughter wanted to leave home so that she could hang about in the streets and have fun. Aïcha told the social worker that she loved her daughter, that she didn't want her to go away, that she was worried about her and that if she came back, everything would be all right. And the social worker and then Jamila ended up believing her. Jamila went back home and before very long the old habits crept back in. My mother criticized the way Jamila behaved, and Jamila was always the 'bad seed'.

Zacarias and I had to butt in now and again, even if it didn't do any good. We often urged our mother: 'Stop, Mum. Why are you talking to her like that? Stop!' She made as if she couldn't hear us. Our stepfather, for his part, was a mere shadow. But our father was getting closer to us. Our mother's strategy as far as he was concerned had changed. She no longer banned us from seeing him. On the contrary, she would often say to us: 'Go on, go out with him, make him pay!' Our father lived from hand to mouth, and when he did have money he was very generous to those around him, but it obviously never occurred to him to give our mother the slightest allowance.

In any event, Zacarias and I decided we would see him regularly. We were fond of him. We didn't really have the feelings of sons, because he hadn't brought us up. But even though he'd been absent, he'd never been mean. He'd never hit us. And for us that was very important. What we really felt for him was sympathy. He was kind to us, he gave us a bit of money and he was funny. He led a slightly chaotic life; he had lots of affairs, and he even took us to discos. One summer's day, just before school started again, he really surprised us. Zacarias and I bumped into him on the Cours Gambetta, beside the canal, a very pleasant spot. We walked with him. He was nattily dressed, wearing a suit and tie, and he told us that he had come to live in Narbonne so that he could see us regularly. As we talked, we walked past an estate agent's, and our father said to us: 'Come with me. I'll show you how you find work when you're really looking for it!' He walked into the office, said hello to the staff, introduced himself as a contractor and asked to see the person running the agency, who, as luck would have it, was available. Then we discovered a facet of our father that we didn't know anything about: he was a self-confident man, sure of his professional worth. He was carrying a small black briefcase from which he took out some photos of his projects. A press book, no less. He told the boss what he could do, listed his job experiences and told him that he'd just arrived in Narbonne. He was his own best salesman, and things fell into place.

A while later, our father was driving a lorry on which was written in large blue letters: 'Entreprise Moussaoui'. With his very direct way of doing things, he had secured work at several building sites. He had bought his equipment and signed up workmen. So for us our father was someone resourceful who earned a good living because he was hard-working, organized and well regarded in his profession. A few years later we were brought down to earth.

One day, when we were walking towards the Narbonne City Hall, a smiling man stopped us in the streets: 'Aren't you the Moussaoui boys?' We actually looked a lot like our father, so we nodded and looked at him at the same time questioningly and vaguely suspiciously. It should be added that our father had once again disappeared into thin air a few months back.

'I knew it was you! I know your father!' added the stranger, breaking into a broad smile.

'Oh, really? You know our father?'

'I'll say! I was in prison with him! I've just got out!'

At first my brother and I didn't react, but we did cast an eye around us to make sure nobody had heard, and above all to make sure that there were no friendss within earshot. And then, once we'd got over our surprise, we started asking the stranger some questions. He told us some very complicated story about money and that our father was in good health: 'He's in good shape, he's a brave guy, and he doesn't get upset about things.' We quite expected that he wouldn't be particularly intimidated by his new cellmates. We'd already seen what happened in Mulhouse, when a man attacked him with a knife: he grabbed the weapon with his bare hands, broke the blade and smashed up his assailant's face.

Back home, we made sure we didn't repeat what we'd just heard about our father, and we managed not to take that episode too seriously. For us, it was just another chance to have a laugh. When we squabbled, one or other of us always whispered to the other, with a big smile: 'Watch out, or I'll tell everyone you're the son of a jailbird!' Tongue in cheek wit, to say the least.

Our mother and our stepfather bought a corner-shop for next to nothing, in an area in the centre of Narbonne that was being renovated. They opened a grocery run by Saïd that took off in no time – primarily because the street had been gradually done up. With her innate business sense, my mother had been clever enough to keep one step ahead of the renovations. What's more, she resold the business and made a pretty profit a while later. She and her partner made enough money to buy a plot of land at Roche-Grise, a fairly sought-after area on the edge of Narbonne. With a small loan of 450,000 francs – roughly 70,000 euros – they began building a large detached house.

Zac and I were really happy at the idea of changing neighbourhoods and leaving the Razimbaud estate and all its petty crime. All the more so because, when you come from that type of neighbourhood, an indelible label inevitably gets stuck to you. For the construction of the house, Saïd dealt with all the major work and then the making good. He handled everything, taking on two labourers to help him and getting Zacarias and me to help out at weekends and in school holidays. We poured cement, mixed plaster, laid breeze-blocks, dug foundations, put up the supporting walls in the basement, laid floors, built brick walls and helped to install the frame... we worked non-stop. Our mother appointed herself site foreman. She didn't know a thing about it, but she was very good at finding out about things. She spent her time visiting colleagues who'd had their houses built, architects to ask them for hints and tips, and builders she knew to glean advice. She repeated over and over to Saïd, who would sometimes suggest another solution: 'It's my house!' Thanks to all of us, 'her' house was built in three months. Saïd probably thought that once it was built it would also be 'his' house. He was wrong.

Our mother said she didn't have enough money to put in central heating, so she had the whole house fitted with electric radiators. We moved in in September, even as the last coat of paint was still drying, but when the first cold snap arrived the plaster was still not completely dry. Damp oozed from every wall. Needless to say, we turned on the radiators and the first electricity bills were huge: our mother tore out her hair, bawled at us, accused us of deliberately wasting electricity, and endlessly told us that we were eating away at all her savings. The atmosphere at home was electric also. As we well knew, for my mother every penny counted. When she was young, this 'sense of economy' was probably logical enough, but little by little money had become the focal point of our family discussions.

Our sisters were accused of far worse things, as well as of being too close to our stepfather. He would sigh and wearily shrug his shoulders. As was his wont, he never said anything. We didn't understand him, we just thought he was weak. In reality, as we later realized, he had just been biding his time – he had another woman, who lived near the grocery, with whom he even had a child. One day, quietly, as ever, he announced as much to my mother, and told her that he was leaving her to be with that other woman.

After Saïd had left our mother, we bumped into him from time to time and our contacts with him were friendly. He had never done us any harm, and we rather liked him, even if none of us had ever put much into the relationship. With Saïd gone, our mother met a few other men, about whom, unfortunately, we knew absolutely nothing.

It has to be admitted that, for us, the house was little more than a place to sleep, which we would go back to every night as late as possible. Real life lay elsewhere. We spent the whole of the following summer at Roche-Grise. It was a residential neighbourhood for architects, engineers and civil servants. Lots of our neighbours had swimming pools and tennis courts and some even had horses. We were the only North Africans in the area, and we didn't make any outward show of wealth. Even so, our mother, a cleaning woman, had succeeded in having her own house built there; it was the sign of a substantial climb up the social ladder.

Roche-Grise had a camping site equipped with table football and ping-pong, so the summer was anything but boring. It didn't take long for us to get together with neighbours of our own age. We went from one swimming pool to another, tried our hand at tennis and even, sometimes, pony-riding...thanks to Zacarias because he very quickly was accepted in this circle. My brother was smart, fun to be around, quick-witted and a charmer. His sense of humour, which was sometimes scathing, would have people laughing until they cried. Those who took a dim view of the Moroccan sons of a cleaning woman invading the middle class circle – and there were some – kept it to themselves. We were athletic, and Razimbaud got us used to dealing out punches, which wasn't necessarily the way the offspring of the middle classes went about things.

In the summer, fifteen or so of us formed a gang that went from pool to pool and tennis court to tennis court. Tennis was a bit like an 'open sesame' in our neighbourhood. Zacarias, who had never before played tennis, very quickly got the hang of it, and thus, he became an acceptable partner. And among our neighbours there were, of course, girls.

Her name was Fanny. A pretty blonde, with white skin and pale eyes. She lived 200 yards from our house. Her brother was one of my friends. Zacarias met her at a friend's house, at their pool. She was fifteen, like him. That meeting would be the start of a real love story, a story that lasted ten years. It was a reciprocal love affair. What Zacarias failed to find in his own home, in his family, he tried to construct elsewhere. Above all, he looked for harmony, gentleness, affection, honesty, loyalty and principles – in a word, a sense of emotional security. He found all that with Fanny.

True, my brother was very secretive and modest by nature. But little by little he told Fanny about his pain and suffering, and about the permanent tension at home with mother. Fanny was his secret garden. He never talked about her, but he spent nearly all his time with her. The only thing was that Fanny came from what some people call a 'good family', a 'good family' that didn't look too kindly on her new friends – and boyfriend. Her father had a high-up job in a big company. He drove a sports car. Her mother was a civil servant. They had a pool too. Fanny's father was racist, in a distressingly predictable way. Fanny's mother knew that her daughter was dating my brother. To start with she didn't say anything. But when her husband found out, she closed ranks with him and they both called Fanny's friendship 'disgraceful'. Previously, Zacarias was just a friend among a bunch of friends, and that made him OK. Now, though, he was the embodiment of a danger threatening their daughter.

That was the time when, as he liked to put it, Zacarias

played at being a 'salmon' – somebody swimming upstream, from the vocational diploma to the baccalauréat, and from the baccalauréat to an advanced vocational certificate. And despite the whirlpools, he got there. So he had every reason to be proud of himself. His girlfriend's parents apparently didn't see things in quite the same way. Up until then, Zacarias acted as if he hadn't realized they didn't approve of him. Like me, he thought some people were racists more because of a lack of culture or out of fear than because of any malice or meanness; as a result, he reckoned they could probably be 'educated'. He was quite sure that Fanny's family would get to know him and change their minds, and that way all the barriers and prejudices against him would come tumbling down. It was a charitable way of looking at things – but way off the mark. So, he was always polite and smiling. But it didn't alter Fanny's parents' feelings one iota – their daughter deserved better than an Arab. And Fanny probably made the mistake of being too honest in telling Zacarias what her parents said about him. Once my brother admitted to himself that they had a basic lack of intelligence, and especially when he realized that no matter what he did Fanny's parents would never change their views, Zacarias started to view them with contempt. He didn't make any effort to be polite any more, and he didn't shrink from letting them see his new attitude. When he went to pick Fanny up for a date, he didn't even go into the garden; instead, he stayed on the pavement outside their house. Actually, that probably suited them fine. As for our mother... Zacarias kept her as far away as he could from his emotional life. He brought Fanny home only when he was absolutely sure their paths wouldn't cross.

At home, things between Zacarias and Aïcha had never been easy. But as the years passed they just got worse. I managed to listen to our mother, bide my time and let the storm pass when shouts and screams filled the house, until she calmed down. I was very fond of her and I reckoned that her tiring job and the lack of consideration that went with it were at times the main cause of her exhaustion and irritability.

Zacarias, though, seemed to have run out of patience completely. He now refused to make any compromises at all. He was more pig-headed than I was, and, above all, he refused to give any ground. For him, keeping quiet for the sake of peace was just cowardice. From the age of fourteen on, he didn't let our mother get away with anything – particularly when he saw her quarrelling with Jamila. One day he sat down opposite me in our bedroom, head in his hands, and told me wearily that he could no longer stand the terrible arguments that rocked the house.

The way he looked at our mother became cold and clinical. Little by little I think he stopped feeling any love for her. He was hard on her. When he talked about her, he called her 'that woman'. He would accuse her of lying.

When they had rows, it was heavy. Zacarias reproached her for living in a fantasy world – imagining things and then thinking that was how things really were. And Zacarias didn't go along with it. The more she lost her temper, the more he made it a point of honour to stay very cool and very cold. That unsettled Aïcha, and he knew it only too well. She would shout louder and louder. He stayed there like marble, staring straight at her and answering: 'It's not true! You're lying! You're making the whole thing up!'

I reacted differently. I reckoned that it served no purpose to put up any resistance to her, to play power games and go against her. In any event, she wouldn't countenance any opinion other than her own. So what was the point? When she believed something, it was futile to try to persuade her that she was wrong, or that she'd misunderstood; she had her beliefs. Nothing would get her to climb down. My tactic, to stop the house turning into a battlefield every day, was to let her shout and say nothing in reply; I would listen to her until her anger subsided. Later, when she'd calmed down, only then would I try to reason with her. I often tried to persuade Zacarias not to be so uncompromising, not to go against her head-on. He would hear me out, but even when he tried to stay calm she provoked him so much that he always rose to the bait. My mother's philosophy was never to try to settle things.

After Jamila, the person she fought most with was Zacarias. She realized that he wasn't afraid of her any longer. There again, she would try to make him think that he wasn't up to things.

I know that these accusations levelled at my mother may seem serious, but they are what really went on. She said violent things. When he heard them, Zacarias would clench his fists and desperately try to keep his cool. It was hard. All the more so because the shouting would go on for hours. A row between my mother and my little brother might start at 6 p.m. and go on until 2 in the morning… My mother gave up only when she saw her son completely at the end of his tether, about to break down. Most of the time Zacarias managed to control himself when he was in her company. Once he'd turned on his heels, he would explode. Sobbing, usually. But never in front of her. I told him the same thing every time: 'You mustn't get into this state. She's our mother, and you can see she's not well. She's tired too; her work's tiring…'

The story of the County Council grants is typical of the sort of crisis there could be at home. Zacarias and I both received students' grants from Aude council. They were meant to cover the cost of school transport. The money came to our mother and she was meant to give it to us each month so that we could pay for the monthly bus pass. But she said we cost her too much money, all round, so she didn't have to give us the bus money. She would either say: 'Sort it out for yourselves' or 'I've already given you the money.'

'How are we supposed to get to school?'

'I've already given you the money.'

'No, you haven't! Give us the money. It's not your money.'

'No, I won't! You're liars. You've already spent the money, I gave it to you before.'

Result: we found ways to take the bus money – our money – from her purse. We didn't have any choice. We had to be at school by eight o'clock and lived four miles away. We tried hitchhiking several times, but it only worked now and then: sometimes we got a ride straight away, but most of the time we were stuck by the roadside, thumbs in the air. Who would pick up two dark-skinned lads at seven in the morning on the way to work? And then in the evening it was the same story on the way home. For a long time I let it all wash over me. And for a long time Zacarias put up with things too. But there was one time when Aïcha played what my brother called a 'real dirty trick' on him. And the row between Zacarias and her was more violent than any they'd ever had before.

It was the day when Zacarias was taking his practical exam for his vocational diploma. He had to be at school by 7.30 a.m. for registration. But the bus didn't come that early. So Zacarias asked our mother to drive him to school that day. She agreed. On the fateful day, Zacarias got up really early and got himself ready. Not a sound in the house. After a while, seeing what time it was, he went and knocked on our mother's bedroom door. No answer. He knocked louder and called her name. Nothing. He went in. Aïcha opened an eye. He said to her: 'Mum, hurry up. I'm going to be late.' She looked at him and said: 'I'm tired. Get yourself to school. Let me sleep.' And she turned towards the wall. He went on at her. She screamed at him: 'Get yourself to school. Leave me in peace!' Zacarias was beside himself. He flew out of the house, slamming every door, hitchhiked and got to school forty-five minutes late. At the end of the exam he still hadn't finished his paper. In a fit, he chucked it into the wastepaper bin. A teacher took pity on him, retrieved his exam paper and handed it in. Thanks to him, Zacarias got his diploma.

But from then on relations between Zacarias and Aïcha became violent. He never forgave her for what she did that day. He was for ever saying about our mother: 'I knew she wouldn't do a thing to help me, but I didn't know she was capable of doing something to hurt me.' Every time they argued, the violence of their words just got worse and worse. Zacarias was pale in the face, but he would snap back at everything she said. He was in control of himself, but maybe he would crack? That's what it looked like, if the expression on his face was anything to go by.

One day, during one of those tiffs, I had no option but to intervene to stop him from hitting her. From then on things went from bad to worse. I advised him to leave home before he really lost it: 'You've got to go, bro. I'll find a solution for you.' I asked a friend who lived in the middle of Narbonne to put him up for a while. So Zacarias left home one morning in 1986. It was meant to be for ever. But he went back home again in 1988, and then left again. After that he didn't return until 1996, eight years later, his head shaved, with a long beard and short trousers. According to my mother, he'd come 'to ask her forgiveness'…

3

LOOKING FOR AN IDENTITY

In the North African community, Zacarias and I had a special status, or, rather, no status at all. At home, Aïcha never talked to us in Arabic. So we felt discriminated against even among the North African community, because we didn't speak its language. Zacarias and I were actually the only members of our family who didn't understand or speak our mother tongue. When we went on at our mother to teach us a few words, she would laugh at our accent and our lousy pronunciation, so we ended up not saying a word. Our sisters, of course, were born in Morocco and went back there almost every year, so they spoke Arabic. The result: when we met Moroccan families, people would feel sorry for us. 'Oh, they don't speak Arabic? *Meskine!* Poor things!' And my mother would respond: 'No, they don't. They're right little French boys, those two.'

Our mother didn't teach us anything, either, about Arab ways and customs, or about Muslim culture. Not because she wasn't acquainted with that culture, but because she didn't want to. What's more, in one of her statements that appeared recently in the media, she said: 'I made sure they didn't hang out with Arabs.'[1] Zac and I asked her several times how you prayed and why. She dodged the issue. She told us it wasn't what people of our age did. Yet since Mulhouse we'd seen our friends going to the mosque with their fathers. So why were we such ignoramuses? We felt ridiculous in the company of others. Who, among the people we knew, might have told us all about these things? Not our father, who wasn't around and in any event he wasn't a practising Muslim. Not our aunts and uncles, either, who all lived on the other side of the Mediterranean. So we decided to ask Saïd, our mother's partner at the time, because he was a practising Muslim.

We saw him bowing, getting up and kneeling back down again. We wanted to know what it all meant, and what the meaning of the words he uttered was. In a kind and slightly awkward way he gave us the relevant books, because he didn't know how to explain all that to us himself. We didn't understand the first thing about it. Those books explained in concrete terms 'how' to pray, but they didn't give us any spiritual information. In Narbonne, in those days, there wasn't a mosque. Instead, there was a 'prayer hall' at St-Jean-St-Pierre, but I didn't know that until much later. And like lots of prayer halls, it wasn't signposted in the street. It was discreet, in an ordinary apartment.

There was no way we could ask our North African friends anything, because that would show up our terrible lack of culture – and they would really have goaded us too. Zac and I found it all a bit disheartening, so we gave up our quest. I was twenty-five when I went into a mosque for the first time. It was in Montpellier. I think the first mosque Zacarias went into was in Great Britain. For Zacarias, who is Muslim by birth, this religious ignorance has had a huge influence on his life. And I think it also had great significance both for people who went to the al-Qaeda training camps in Pakistan and for French prisoners at Guantanamo Bay.

At this juncture I'd like to interrupt the chronology of our story and say one or two things that seem crucial to me for any understanding of Zacarias's subsequent actions.

★

There are now more than one billion people in the world who adhere to Islam. Ninety-five per cent of them are Sunnites. Four per cent are Shiites. Slightly more than a million – i.e. one per cent – are called Wahhabis. But this particular million are sitting on a financial windfall because they are backed by Saudi Arabia, the world's largest oil reserves.

To get a closer idea of the influence of Wahhabism in the world, the international context must be examined. The present-day state of things is dramatic, be it the war in Chechnya and its appalling massacres, or the end of the war waged by the Russians in Afghanistan. Right away, Zacarias and I felt tremendous admiration for the late Commandant Massoud, a hero of that war. Bosnia, at that time, was undergoing 'ethnic cleansing', which we tend to regard as a systematic extermination – genocide taking place before our very eyes. As for Algeria, this is something of a special case in this litany of bloodshed – more than 100,000 dead in ten years. A civilian population massacred. Lastly, Palestine is under occupation, and the Palestinians live under a system of apartheid.

For any young North African living in France, all this horror is intolerable and exacerbates feelings that are already greatly bruised by overtly expressed discrimination against Arabs and Muslims. We are actually easy prey because many people have understood the drama we're living through. What's more, no voices are being raised to give vent to and defend our feelings. One-track thinking rules and nobody dares speak out against all the horror.

In Montpellier Zacarias made friends with students who came from a tough neighbourhood called the Petit-Bard, and from a housing estate, the Paillade. These students explained to him that what was going on in Algeria was a legitimate struggle against corrupt leaders and injustices and that the fighters in this struggle were called the *mujaheddin*. Their analysis seemed very odd to us: Algeria being a land of Islam, how could you make war in the name of Islam against other Muslims? Women, children, young men and old, alike, throats slit with saws or beheaded with axes. That couldn't have been done in the name of Islam. All these atrocities were to be condemned in no uncertain terms.

Nowadays, in France, when a young Muslim becomes interested in learning about his religion and wants to find out about his parents' values and the history of the community he's a part of, and when his parents can't provide answers to his questions, he tends to turn to an Arab cultural or religious association. He will probably go to look things up in Arab–Muslim bookshops as well as in more traditional bookshops. In the latter, the material on offer is often quite expensive and geared to a readership that tends to be quite intellectual. Furthermore, the books are often written by Orientalists. The Arab–Muslim bookshops, on the other hand tend to be friendlier and more easy-going, and the books are less expensive. You can find plenty of things reminiscent of your parents' culture – the same perfume, the same clothes, *soubhahs*[2] and *siwaks*[3] – as well as magazines, tapes and videos for learning Arabic, the Koran, books about the foundations of Islam, religious practices, the history of the Arab world and Arab–Muslim culture. There are plenty of these books, in every shape and size.

The Muslim may also be approached by *tablighs*[4] whom he can meet by chance in the street or at the lectures and gatherings at the fair organized by the French Union of Islamic Organizations. At this fair he will find all kinds of products: clothes, perfumes… anything and everything that can be traded. In addition, there are religious courses given in centres run by the Association of Islamic Welfare Projects in France which also organizes the celebration of religious festivals, such as the commemoration of the birth of the Prophet Muhammad. The landscape for a young novice is like uncultivated soil, waiting to be planted. People don't necessarily agree with each other. During the meetings, people may bring up trivial and secondary subjects year after year, making others think that they are the crucial questions. Quite by chance you may stumble upon an extremely vitriolic book or a tremendously moderate book. It is also possible to come upon authentic religious instruction... or upon political and sectarian indoctrination.

In the absence of any informed parent and clearly defined religious authority, the young novice is thus left to his own devices. And danger lurks everywhere. A number of preachers and speakers talking in the name of religion are in no way qualified to do so. The main criteria for recruiting imams are quite simply a knowledge of Arabic and an ability to step up into the pulpit to speak... Sometimes they are required to know the Koran by heart, but nobody ever asks any questions about the real nature of their theological studies. The first generation of immigrants had two concerns: finding places of worship in which to pray and having someone available to teach Arabic and the Koran to their children. But when the people with these responsibilities are novices, the criteria insisted upon are, on the whole, less demanding...

Young students who call themselves members of the 'Muslim Brotherhood', *Hizb Attahrir* (the Party of Liberation) or Wahhabis set themselves up as fierce rivals to this generation of imams by being active in associations where they organize Arabic lessons, tutoring and religious instruction. Sometimes they even work alongside these imams, gradually taking over their role as educators of children and young people. These young students thus manage to be in contact with the young members of the second generation of immigrants, and organize meetings and conferences. Hitherto, serious and moderate traditional religious instruction has been almost non-existent.

At the same time, for a young, French-speaking Muslim, plenty of bookshops are overflowing with works by Sayyid

Qotb, A-Mawdoudi, Al-Qaradawi, Muhammad ibn Abd Al-
Wahhâb, Ibn Baz and Al-Outhaymine. All the leading figures
of Wahhabism and the 'Muslim Brotherhood', who are also
known as Qotbists. What is there to be found in these books?
One or two selected excerpts may be instructive:

> Today, a Muslim society no longer exists,
> there is no more Islam and there are no
> more Muslims. Muslim society will only
> come back into being when existing
> regimes have been destroyed and given way
> to a power which respects divine legislation
> to the letter. All the societies in the world,
> with no exceptions, are idolatrous and full
> of infidels, conscious that authority belongs
> solely to God. For when a man dares to
> invent laws, he proclaims himself the equal
> of God. And all peoples which subject
> themselves to such a man without
> resistance or rebellion are in a state of
> adoration of him, by their obedience to
> him. The true Muslim today is the Muslim
> who makes jihad against all governments
> whose legislation is human in origin, in
> order to topple them and reinstate divine
> legislation.[5]

You can also read in this book:

> There is but one house, it is the house of
> Islam which contains the Muslim state, any
> other house [where this authority is non-
> existent, which is the case everywhere, even
> in Islamic lands (author's note)] is merely
> hostility for the Muslim and his relationship
> with it must only be war or else an armistice
> with special conditions; it can hardly be

> regarded as the house of Islam and there can
> be no friendly understanding between its
> inhabitants and Muslims.[6]

Hatred oozes from every page. These statements are the outward manifestation of an embittered and even sectarian state of mind, and they are accordingly dangerous.

One of the symbolic figures of the violence which is a hallmark of the followers of Wahhabism and Qotbism is called Ayman Al-Zawahiri. Who is this Egyptian, who is known as bin Laden's right-hand man? He came into the public eye when the Al-Jazeera television station broadcast one or two video cassettes of bin Laden. Ayman Al-Zawahiri was arrested and imprisoned in 1981 following the assassination of the Egyptian president Anwar el-Sadat. He has also, since 1991, been the leader of the Egyptian organization called 'Al-Jihad'. This movement is reckoned to be one of the most extremist and murderous there is. In fact, in 1992 alone the terrorist operations it carried out brought about the deaths of 1,200 people in Egypt. You recognize a tree by its fruit! What does Ayman Al-Zawahiri say about the influence that the writings of Sayyid Qotb have had on him?

In December 2001, in *Asharq-i-Awsat*, the Arabic periodical published in London, appeared extracts of a manuscript of Ayman Al-Zawahri:

> Dr Ayman Al-Zawahri, leader of the Egyptian
> Al-Jihad organization and a right-hand man
> of Osama bin Laden in the Al-Qaida
> organization, talks about Sayyid Qotb...the
> Jihadist movement in Egypt embarked on its
> struggle against the government in the 1960s,
> when president Gamal Abdel Nasser
> conducted his campaign against the 'Muslim
> Brotherhood'. With the execution of the most

important of the 'Muslim Brotherhood' leaders, Sayyid Qotb, the powers-that-be thought that they had managed to rid Egypt of the Islamic movement. But that act was the detonator that sparked the Jihadist movement against the Egyptian government. Sayyid Qotb made possible the establishment of the Brotherhood in his explosive book *Milestones on the Road*, which gave rise to the revival of fundamentalism. The group that had been led by Sayyid Qotb decided to aim its attacks against the powers then in place, because these powers were the enemy of Islam and had strayed from the way approved by Allah in refusing to comply with his Law. Sayyid Qotb's call was – and is – the spark fuelling the Islamic revolution against the enemies of Islam both within and without, and bloody episodes occurred day after day. This revolution assumed a greater resolve in its belief, a refined precision in its strategy, a richer understanding of the nature of the struggle, and more experience in relation to the obstacles encountered. Sayyid Qotb played an important part in guiding Muslim youth along this path, in the latter half of the twentieth century, in Egypt in particular and in Arab regions in general and he became a model of veracity and an example of perseverance. The apparently still waters on the surface hid beneath them seething uprisings fomented by the ideas and the call of Sayyid Qotb, and the formation of the contemporary Jihadist cells in Egypt.

It is difficult to deny that Wahhabi and Qotbist ideologies are behind numerous murders, assassinations, attacks, massacres and many civil wars. In the recent past, there were massacres at Mecca, Medina and At-Ta'if, as well as in Jordan, Iraq, Kuwait and the United Arab Emirates. Even today, there are still massacres in Algeria, and yet the leaders of organizations which are well established in the Western world and the Near East openly claim to follow this ideology. They describe Wahhabi ideology and that of Sayyid Qotb as a reformist ideology and they declare their loyalty to it. When they introduce Wahhabi or Qotbist ideologies, they assert that this literature contains 'many pages of great beauty'. When they talk about massacres of local populations, it is never to denounce them vigorously, but rather to talk down their scale. For them, what is involved is 'a warlike undertaking during which they [the Wahhabis (author's note)] at times have violently attacked all those who refused to follow them'. What is more, Wahhabis and Qotbists alike justify this recourse to violence by the fact that they are driven by a desire for Islamic renewal and reform. So the world is full of people who make use of this pretext of Islamic renewal and reformism, in particular Fayçal Mawlawi, Fathi Yakan and Yusuf Al-Qaradawi. In France it is most often the followers of the French Union of Islamic Organizations and of Tarek Ramadan who exploit this theme of reformism.

This so-called 'reformism' arouses neither anxiety nor suspicion. For many it is a synonym of progress and modernity. A number of people actually understand the term 'reform' as an improvement introduced into the moral and social arena. But this is just a monstrous sham and this is why it's important to uncover its mechanisms. Herein, in fact, lie all the symptoms of double-speak. Concepts of reform and reformism, as they are known in France, refer back to the historical context of the sixteenth century when Protestantism was founded. Reformism was advocated in France and elsewhere in the world against the Catholic Church. This term also conjures up an opposition to a Catholic clergy which was accused of every conceivable vice, including bearing responsibility for the problems of society. The religious institution was suspected of having fossilized both society and religious thinking. The Qotbists play very insistently on this feeling in the Western world, and in French society in particular. Protestantism is a de facto phenomenon in Anglo-Saxon countries, and has spread a great deal. France, since the Revolution, has been dominated by the concept of laicism. So there is a culture, not to say reflexes, which inevitably elevates anyone who appropriates concepts of reform and reformism.

People who are prepared to be won over, or who are at best interested, by reformism in the Muslim world may have several motivations. Some of them like to see the influence of their society in the Muslim community, or they like to think they have contributed something to this Muslim world. This pseudo-influence takes shape in economic, political and strategic fields. And it irks them to see Muslims barricade themselves behind their customs and their values. For others, the idea of reform is seductive when applied to the Muslim world. In fact, this concept enables them to hope to see Muslim society changing by setting aside traditional religious institutions, in the same way that Europeans have managed to do by ousting the Catholic Church. Because for them the ousting of religion from the public domain of society represents a step forward. If we want to make things diagrammatic, their double-speak breaks down into two parts.

On the one hand, they cultivate the hope of Western reformists who wish to see signs of their influence in Muslim countries. It is for this reason, moreover, that so-called Muslim reformists lay claim to borrowings from Western society's science and modernity.

On the other hand, the writings of Wahhabi and Qotbist

thinkers hold out no such promise. On the contrary, they advocate the destruction of all society and the massacre of populations obedient to laws which are not taken from their reading of Muslim tradition. Their discourse is all the more distorted because it takes as its target traditional Islam, in the guise of reformism. Qotbists thus introduce Sunnite theologians as those who stop their writings from engaging human intelligence. They accuse Sunnite theologians of engaging in futile and fossilized factional debates. The goal of this strategy is to do away with those who are actually the only bulwarks against extremism and fanaticism within the Muslim community.

Let's take Al-Qaradawi, for example, one of the leading lights in the Wahhabi–Qotbist line of thinking. He has a pretty high media profile. He hosts programmes on religious topics on the Al-Jazeera TV channel. According to certain sources, he's also a board member of a bank called At-Taqwa, mentioned in the funding of terrorist organizations. He also features on brochures produced by the French Union of Islamic Organizations and has even been one of the guests of honour of its 2000 Le Bourget conference in Paris, where he delivered a lecture. What does he write?

Al-Qaradawi criticizes the apprenticeship and instruction of what are known as legal subjects. In his book *The Worship of God in Islam*, he has this to say: 'Let's leave aside the lengthy, hollow and complicated arguments which fill our law books by making distinctions between pillars,[7] conditions,[8] obligations, sunna [habitual practices], recommendations, revocations and unadvisable matters.' He adds: 'The specialist scholar is permitted to study these terms in this way, provided that it is for himself. But to teach this to ordinary people is, of course, an obvious mistake.'[9]

This fatwa advocated by Al-Qaradawi is representative of a desire to denigrate and discredit traditional Muslim instruction. But to replace it with what? With an ideology of terror. Al-Qaradawi thus defends extremists who kill Muslims and take their goods. Here he sees a deep-seated attachment to religion. In his book *The Tendency to Exaggeration in Excommunication*, he writes: 'It is this extremism that has prompted these sincere young people, who are attached to their religion, to excommunicate those opposed to them among Muslims, to kill them and take their goods.' But these terrorists have tarnished and distorted the image of Islam in people's minds. How can their criminality, their terrorism and their extremism convey a profound attachment to religion? How can Al-Qaradawi dare say that they are 'sincere'?

It is easy to see how the pseudo-reformists, with their double-speak, get the Western world to believe that they are allies. Let us here interject the tale of the scorpion which, to cross a river, asked a tortoise to carry it on his back. He repeated to him that they were allies, with the same interests at heart, and that it would be suicidal for the scorpion to harm the tortoise as they crossed the river. The tortoise agreed and took the scorpion on its back, but once in mid-stream the scorpion gave the tortoise a fatal sting. And when the dying tortoise asked, 'Why did you do that? Now we're both going to die', the scorpion replied, 'I can't help it. It's the way I am.' So Wahhabis use the Western world to attack the Muslim world, but the West is also their victim.

In France the situation is especially alarming because to support Wahhabis and Qotbists, the 'Muslim Brotherhood' party, against the representatives of traditional Islam is to undermine those effectively and actively fighting against extremism. It is important to lend an ear to Muslims following the instruction of the four traditional Sunnite schools (Malikite, Chafiite, Hanafite and Hanbalite). It is actually these Muslims who, within the Muslim community in France and in the world, backed up by arguments and proof, demonstrate and unveil the falsehoods that Wahhabis and Qotbists are trying to put over. To gain an ear within the

Muslim community, these latter cultivate the illusion of truth and do their utmost to give the appearance of religious legality. They also claim to use terms that have powerful positive connotations within the Muslim community: for example, the terms 'Muslim Brotherhood' and 'Salafites'. In reality, however, this use of such terms is improper and unjustified, and it involves no more than a usurpation, whose goal is to lead the neophyte astray. This is why it is crucial that the representatives of Sunnite Islam wage a determined intellectual struggle. Obviously, it would be suicidal for our society to sideline those who are the first line of defence against extremism and fanaticism.

4

UPROOTED AND CAST OUT

Let's get back to our story and deal with the dislocation rift
we were experiencing. In our youth, Zac and I hardly knew
anything about Morocco. We'd been there twice, once in 1974
and again in 1977. I was only ten when we made that last visit
and my brother was eight. So we hardly knew our family: our
grandmother, our aunt, our uncles, and all our cousins, girls
and boys. Our grandmother had visited us, once, in Mulhouse, when we were very young. We had very few memories
of her.

As we were of an age when we could understand things,
our mother painted a very negative picture of that family that
was so alien to us. She said that her mother, Amina, our
grandmother, was mean-spirited. She reproached her brother
Muhammad and her sister Zouhour for being too dedicated
to bringing up their children. In any event, it was as if
Zacarias and I didn't have a grandmother, or an uncle, or an
aunt, or any cousins, because, unlike our sisters, we never saw
any of them. Nadia and Jamila would go with my mother on
her trips to Morocco. They've got a family. We don't! My
mother took Nadia with her because she was proud of her.
And she took Jamila along because she was trying to get her
married off in the village. One summer she even left her with
her brother so that he could marry her off. But it didn't work.

Sometimes my mother said things which, were they to come from the mouth of a born-and-bred French person, could be taken as xenophobic. But even if my mother seemed keen to forget that she was an Arab, she still was. What she wanted was to live the way she wanted to, without constraints, and making sure that her sons did not have any contact with that world from which she nevertheless had come.

She had another habit which also cut us off a bit more from our Mediterranean roots: we didn't celebrate Muslim festivals and holidays. Moroccans are often merry, fervent believers in celebrating Ramadan, the *Mawlid*, which marks the birth of the Prophet, or the *Eid el-kebir* – the Celebration of Abraham's Sacrifice. On the other hand, at Roche-Grise, when we were already well into our teens, my mother started to celebrate Christmas. All our North African friends at school seemed quite happy to celebrate these Muslim festivals, whereas we hardly knew what they meant... But what we understood only too well was that our family wasn't like any other. We didn't feel like born-and-bred French people, and we realized as much every time we came up against racism. We didn't live like Moroccans, either.

Thus a void insidiously formed in us, an abyss which Zacarias and I would both try to negotiate, but in different ways. Like many young people of our generation, we were aware that we were not well acquainted with our original culture. We knew nothing about almost all the social codes of the Arab world. And yet we were not truly accepted in the country of our birth. Native French people rarely think twice about making us feel that we're not altogether 'like them'. This feeling gnawed away at us. And when we did manage to forget about it, it took just one word to bring it back to the surface: 'integration'.

Throughout our youth this word rang in our ears. To start with, we simply didn't understand what it was about. We were born here, on this earth, in this country. We had grown up

here. So what did 'integration' mean? What concept did this
term encompass? How were we to become 'integrated' in
French society when we were French? Growing up, making
the shift from childhood to adolescence, and then from
adolescence to adulthood, in these conditions, is very
upsetting for people who have trouble finding a place for
themselves. If, in addition to this identity crisis, he doesn't
have a harmonious family life, then the human being feels that
he belongs 'to nothing'; he feels like an unstable electron, in a
world that is faithless and lawless.

My first recollection of someone hurling a racist remark in
our faces goes way back to when we were eight and ten years
old. We were living in Mulhouse at 8 Rue de Kaysersberg. At
the foot of our apartment block there was a large, green play
area: for us, this was an ideal playground. Every day after
school, Zac and I would play marbles with the same friend,
who was a neighbour. A few months after we'd gone back to
school after the summer, one afternoon, at about 4.30, he
appeared as usual. We called out to him: 'Rémi!' He didn't
budge. He looked at us. From afar. We walked over to him to
ask him what was the matter.

'I can't play with you.'

'How come? Why can't you play with us?'

'Because my parents said I can't.'

'But why have your parents said you can't play with us
today? We play marbles together every day.'

'No, it's not just today, it's for always. They say that you're
niggers, and they don't want me to play with niggers.'

Zacarias and I looked at each other, more surprised than
hurt. Rémi looked more or less as stunned as we did. He was
clearly aware that the words he'd just spoken were serious. But
he probably didn't really understand them. Nor did we. We
were still kids. Even if we intuitively knew what those words
meant, we were still unable to decipher them. All the more so
because we knew very well that we were not 'niggers'! That's

one of the old memories of racism which keeps haunting me. Little by little we would grow used to it...

At La Fontaine, one of the teachers had a visceral hatred for North Africans. Incredible as it might seem, he did not hide his attitude. When he came across a student of Arab origins in the lavatory, he would hit him. All the students knew that this went on, but nobody said anything. Zacarias got hit, I got hit, and others did too. In silence. It was *omertà*. As if it only had to do with the teacher and us. As if this was the rule of a game laid on us by a racist teacher. Our goal was to be one step ahead of him, and never to be in the lavatory when he was there.

In this sort of situation, a child doesn't really understand what's happening to him. He doesn't know why people are nasty. He simply knows that there are nasty people about. This is life's apprenticeship. And then, when the child grows up, he learns how not to let it get to him. He learns to use his fists. And when he can lash out, he lashes out. He also learns how to pick out people with prejudices. It's as if a tremendous inner radar system is set in motion, but unfortunately it doesn't work all the time – far from it. This is why most young kids on housing estates know how to fight. This isn't necessarily the case with young people who live in smart neighbourhoods.

When we were faced with racism as children, Zacarias and I would go straight and tell our mother. It was one of the rare things that seemed to get to her. She would be outraged, and say over and over: 'They're all racists! They're all racists!' But what could she do? There's something exasperating and extremely frustrating about displays of ordinary racism. If you catch someone in the act, perhaps with witnesses, if you can't produce an immediate reaction you're on your own, chewing over your bitterness and feeling guilty, after the fact, for not saying or doing the right thing. But it's already too late, there's nothing to be done. So our mother couldn't go and see the supermarket cashier to accuse her of saying something out of place to us. At best, the cashier would deny it; at worst, she'd create a fuss.

Later on, as young teenagers, we had different reactions. The girls we went out with would often tell us that their parents disapproved of us and didn't want their daughters hanging out with Arabs. We would just shrug it off. For us, when we were thirteen and fourteen, the way grown-ups saw things didn't matter to us. And we refused to waste our energy thinking about such problems, for which, in any event, we knew intuitively we would never find any solutions.

The rise of Le Pen in the political landscape marked a turning point in the history of racism in France. Until the National Front started getting control of town halls, until it chalked up an amazing score in the 1984 European elections, nobody really ever dreamed of saying they were a racist. Certain French people were, but they were ashamed to admit it. But when Le Pen started started to get so many votes, some French people stopped hiding their real beliefs. Those openly proclaiming what they thought became more and more numerous: 'France is for the French, we're fed up with immigrants. To hell with wogs, niggers and yids.' Louder and louder they claimed 'the right to be racist', like the prerogative of a wholesome brand of freedom! It was a 180-degree about-turn. And France would suffer the consequences of it much later on, in the 2002 presidential elections…

Up until that time, there had been little or no idea that so much racism existed, along with a spirit of exclusion. But when certain people, in certain French towns and cities, started announcing that they loathed foreigners, the fact was that the terms of reference had changed. 'Liberté, Égalité, Fraternité' no longer meant anything. We realized that there was double-speak: there was the language of official speeches, and the language of reality. And for us this had serious consequences. It wasn't a hunch any more, it was a certainty:

we weren't French 'like the others'. Or, worse still, we weren't French at all. And yet we were French, we were born in France, we grew up in France, we went to school in France, we spent our childhood and teenage years in France, we had friends in France and we worked in France.

The years just before you become a teenager are when you start dealing with the bureaucracy on your own – for example, putting together a family dossier for the registrar's office. The form was headed with the words FRENCH NATIONALITY. But more often than not, the official behind the window asked Zac and me what our nationality was.

Not only were we aware of being French in a way that was 'not like the others', but we were also aware that we weren't like all other Moroccans either. The little we did pick up about that other society was from our friends, never from our family. But we did want to look like Sofiane, Khaled and Muhammad. Every time we went back to school, it always bothered us having to say whether we spoke French or Arabic at home. But on the other hand we didn't appreciate our 'differentness' not being taken into account at school. Our history and geography lessons always gave us a one-sided view of Arabs and Muslims. In history, they talked to us about the Algerian war – the war between the French and the Arabs!

The school cafeteria was also a place of petty, day-to-day aggro. For even if we didn't know anything about religion, we still didn't eat pork. Every day, all year round, we were obliged to ask the question: 'Do you have anything other than pork?' And every day, the whole year long, we would get the same response: 'Why?'

'Because I'm a Muslim. I don't eat pork.'

'Oh for heaven's sake! Can't you Muslim people be like everybody else?'

There was one day when a pea and bacon dish was on the menu. When I protested, one of the kitchen staff took my plate, stabbed furiously at the bits of bacon as he pulled them out and handed me back my plate, grumbling: 'You're not going to bug us over a few bits of bacon.' A classmate who was not a Muslim snapped back at him: 'And how would you like it if someone put a few ounces of shit on your plate?' Once again we felt under attack. In fact we were just confused. We couldn't recognize ourselves either in the all-French model or in the North African model.

Millions of young North Africans and other Africans feel just what Zacarias and I have felt. For children, their social life really starts at school – what teachers and staff think is incredibly important for them. If children don't feel respected or accepted, they have trouble building a positive image of themselves.

And all it would take would be for the state school system to make a little effort to adapt things for students of Muslim origin so that they could feel a bit less skinned alive. The country must be capable of making this kind of effort, even if only for society no longer to turn out people who can't find their place in it and who grow up suffering as a result. Suffering doesn't help people to think. Pain cannot be intellectualized, it is suffered. And when it is externalized, it is already late in the day: the lack of bench marks, the aggressiveness and malaise among all these young people can explode in the form of petty delinquency. Or worse...

As kids in Mulhouse, Zacarias and I often said that there really were many racists in France. In Narbonne, the xenophobia took on another form and gave rise to sheer violence. In the summer there were village fairs all over the region. We were seventeen and eighteen by then. Needless to say, these fairs gave us a chance to have some fun and meet girls. We would happily go to them, usually hitchhiking. One night, with two other friends, we went to the Coursan fair, a few miles north of Narbonne. The fair was held in the middle of the town stadium, with several stages and bands. We left there running for our lives through the vineyards, being chased by a bunch of young village kids who wanted to beat up some wogs. How many times, when Zacarias and I went to village fairs, just a few miles from Narbonne, did we have to leave like that, running through the vineyards? For us it was a question of escaping from what were potentially very real attacks. Sometimes, it was probably just young kids who'd drunk six or seven beers and just wanted to hit somebody. Luckily, we also sometimes managed to scare them off. There's often strength in numbers. But those were fights during which fists often flew thick and fast.

In Narbonne in 1989, on the night of 14 July, an unfortunate thing happened which marked us for good, causing us to feel extremely uneasy and very suspicious towards institutions. It was late, getting on to midnight, when I left some friends who had asked me out to supper. They dropped me off just before it was time for the fireworks in the town square, not far from where my brother and some other friends were waiting for me near the canal. It's a very touristy spot, with lots of bars and outdoor terraces. I had a hundred yards to walk. I was walking quietly along when a guy tapped me on the shoulder from behind. I turned around and looked at him. He could have been twenty-five or thirty, but I don't really know. He said to me: 'Come over here, will you? I've got a couple of things to say to you. Follow me.' I found his behaviour weird, so I ignored him and continued walking. But I wasn't worried because there were lots of people around.

After ten or fifteen yards I felt a hand grabbing me from behind again. I turned around, a bit annoyed, but not really bothered, and – pow! – the guy landed a right, full in my face. I fell back into a flower-bed. I was completely groggy, but I got up and saw the guy coming to hit me again. I took to my heels, panicked because I didn't know who he was or why he wanted to hit me. But in my panic I went the wrong way and ran further from where my brother was waiting for me. I crossed the street, passed the edge of the square and noticed six or seven cops. I ran straight up to them shouting: 'There's a guy running after me to hit me! Look what he's done!' My face was covered in blood. And the cops looked at me suspiciously as I gabbled away. At that very moment the guy appeared and went for me, but I dodged him, crying out to the cops: 'That's him, that's him!' At that, one of the cops pulled out a tear gas canister. With one hand he grabbed me by the hair and with the other he emptied the tear gas right in my face. I was stunned, my eyes were burning, I was suffocating, so I decided to run away, but I managed to go only another hundred yards, and then I collapsed in a faint, outside a restaurant. Some friends of mine were eating inside, luckily for me. Because just as they came out to help me, the guy appeared again. To finish me off. My friends, obviously enough, got in his way and he ran off. They took me to hospital. My face was burned by the tear gas. I was in a state of shock, not so much because of the crazy guy who probably just wanted to 'bash a wog', as by the way the cop had behaved. I was a victim. I was asking him for help, and he gassed me.

My mother came to see me at the hospital. She was just as shocked as I was and insisted that I not let this incident go unnoticed, that I lodge a complaint against the guy who'd hit me and the cop who'd gassed me. So the following morning I went with my mother to the police station to lodge a complaint. And – would you believe it? We couldn't do anything. Impossible to lodge a complaint. First of all, the policeman on duty kept on saying: 'You know, in the thick of things, it's really impossible to say what's going on...' And then, seeing that we were determined, he ended up by losing his temper and telling us to get out, shouting all the while: 'We've got better things to do. Just count yourself lucky that it didn't go any further. Now clear off!' My mother and I were furious and disgusted.

Later on, a lawyer friend told me that it's possible to lodge a

complaint directly with the state prosecutor. I know people in
'SOS Racism', and that association backed my complaint to
make sure it wouldn't be buried. In the end, there was actually
a trial: the guy admitted that he had hit me for no reason. He
was given a suspended seven-day prison sentence and a 2,500
franc[1] fine. As for the cop, I never heard what happened to him.

Zacarias suffered just as much as, if not more than I did
from that incident. It really enraged us. Can you imagine the
frustration of being the victim of an assault, trying to get help
from the forces of law and order, and realizing that the people
that you expect to help you do you in? The cop didn't just gas
and insult me. It was worse than that. For him, quite
obviously, when an Arab and a native Frenchman are
involved, it's always the Arab who's guilty. That kind of thing
can really fill a person's heart with hatred for a long time.

The hatred faded, but our mistrust remained. Especially in
my brother. For us, from that moment on, it was obvious that
there were fascists in the police force. Later on, with a little
thought, I rationalized things. I'm well aware that there's no
point in making sweeping conclusions from just one incident.
But still today when I have a problem, my initial reflex is not
to go to the cops for help.

One night, a few years later, Zacarias went to a disco with
his girlfriend. I tried to talk him out of going because I knew all
too well the risks he would face going to this club. Every time
we tried to get into that place, it ended in humiliation. Just
trying to get in was a problem. Most times we were turned
away: 'No entry ugly mugs.' To avoid such unpleasant scenes, I
decided not to go there any more. But Zac was pig-headed. If
he wanted to go to a club with Fanny, he went. That night they
got in without any trouble: they were a couple, and the bouncer
let them through. But inside things weren't so good. Zacarias
and Fanny danced a slow number together. A guy tapped on
my brother's shoulder and punched him even before Zac had
turned around. Blood poured out of his mouth. Zacarias lashed

back with a head butt and the guy fell to the floor. A second guy came up, Zac broke his collar-bone with his elbow. A third guy got involved, and then my brother really got beaten up. And all the time he's being hit, what does he hear? 'Had it with these niggers! They're even taking our women!' Throughout the brawl, Fanny was beside Zacarias, sobbing and afraid for him. In the end, the bouncers moved in, took Zac with them and stayed close by him until the club closed. They even went so far as to take Zac and Fanny back home by car, in case the others were waiting outside to finish him off. Next day, Zac's eyes were swollen and his mouth misshapen. I couldn't help but tell him: 'I told you not to go there!'

One of the three guys who attacked Zacarias was at the same school as us. He was a rugby player. Needless to say, that Monday morning, as Zac's big brother, I was duty bound to intervene after what he'd put Zacarias through a couple of nights before. It was only thanks to the spontaneous help of another student, who was spurred on – he would tell me later – by the unequal nature of the fight, that I didn't have my face smashed in in turn – the rugby player was twice my size. Two of us only just managed to deal with him. From that moment on, hatred smouldered between us until the end of the year. In any event, the atmosphere was very tough. Now, some of the students admitted openly to being racists. Actually, the word is not well chosen, because they didn't 'admit' it – they boasted about it, which showed the alarming way in which attitudes were evolving.

In tandem with this poisoned atmosphere, before very long there was the problem of finding a way into the job market. As young French men of North African origin, we had a sense of deep-seated injustice. We had good school results, but, when it came to finding jobs as trainees in companies, things were not easy. Some bosses were quite frank about it; their line was: 'I don't want any Arabs.' It goes without saying that there were never any witnesses to this kind of remark. Others reacted in a different way: 'I'm very sorry, but we've just taken someone on.' Oddly enough, though, the very next day, a classmate would tell you he got the job you were after. What were you to think? This is one of the really perverse side-effects of racism – there are times when you have doubts about yourself and your analytical abilities. You no longer know if you didn't get that job because your qualifications are not as good as those of your classmate, or because of your Arab face. The playing field is never level, and you can easily become paranoid.

Zacarias came up against this problem even more acutely than I did, because he was in the first vocational class – 'Automated Mechanical Systems Maintenance' – in Narbonne. Over a two-year period he had to put in sixteen trainee weeks in firms. Students had to find a firm that would agree to train them. As a rule, they found their work experience placements through acquaintances, by pulling strings or by luck. For Zacarias and for all the other students of North African and African origin, a handful of teachers, who were well aware of the problem, managed to find them placements. One teacher, Mr Dupont was a wonderful man: Zacarias and I didn't need to explain to him that we were having trouble finding jobs because we were Arabs. He guessed as much himself, but he also didn't tell us that he would help us: discretion on the part of victim students, and discretion on the part of a realistic teacher. We knew he understood. It was both a relief and a real day-to-day burden. Every day we went to work, and every day we might have to face this problem.

Not to mention the racism among certain teachers themselves. Zacarias had a teacher he grumbled about all the time. His colleagues were aware that he was a racist, but it was an insidious, underhand kind of racism, expressed in the form of marks and remarks on the school reports. Zacarias talked to me and to Fanny about this, nobody else. What was he to do? He was powerless. When Zacarias was faced with humiliation, he reacted in a different way from the way I did. He locked himself away in his suffering, he nurtured it, it gnawed away at him quietly. And when it was I who was a victim of racism, instead of him, the result was just the same: he suffered in his heart and soul, almost more than I did. So Mr Dupont helped Zacarias whenever he looked for jobs, and he would help me too the following year. It was he, too, who got Zac recruited as supervisor at the Victor-Hugo secondary school, so my brother had a roof over his head and food on his plate.

Even today, within the state educational system, some people elect to deny the problem of racism and discrimination. The first time I saw this topic broached head-on by a teacher was when I myself was a supply teacher. In the middle of an electro-technical certificate meeting, a colleague took the floor: 'How do I manage to find courses for my North African students, when I have bosses who say to me: "We don't want any Arabs?"' The answer, given by the school inspectors is straightforward: 'There are laws in France against racial discrimination.' Which thus means that racism in the workplace is still a reality, but the great difference is that it is cracked down on by the law and that, nowadays, you can speak out about it openly.

5

ZAC'S DREAM: A PLACE IN THE SUN

At the end of the summer of 1986, it was my turn to leave Roche-Grise. I told my mother I was going to be with Zacarias, and live with him, and that it would be better for my kid brother not to be on his own any more. She didn't say anything at the time. Zac and I had temporary work as labourers all summer: building roads, cleaning drains under bridges... It was a very physical work, and it enabled us to put a bit of money aside. I begged my mother to come with me to rent a studio apartment close to the main square in Narbonne. Not so that she would pay the deposit, but just to let the owner see I was totally committed. What a surprise! She agreed. So we rented the studio and found our independence and peace of mind. But this luxury had its price – the rent.

We had to fend for ourselves and find odd jobs. In material terms, life very quickly became harder. Luckily, we could eat in the cafeteria. Zacarias got his vocational certificate. From then on it was decided that he really would 'swim against the current': this expression seemed right for him because he would have to swim upstream to get back into an academic curriculum. For my part, I was in the last year of my electrical engineering certificate.

In the evenings, in our studio, our diet consisted of pasta

and potatoes. Sometimes friends invited us to eat with them – we never refused. We were led by our stomachs: 'Let's go and see so-and-so. His fridge is always full.' We felt more than a bit guilty quite often. But Zacarias refused to ask mother for help. Fanny attended to my brother's every need. As often as she could, she brought him bags full of food, and in particular lots of fruit juice for the vitamins. Now and then he would share things with me, when he was in a good mood. Day-to-day living wasn't easy, and we argued more often than before, usually over silly little things.

Winter came. Luckily, the strikes resulting from the university reform proposals would help us to get through the winter – we offered our apartment as headquarters of the Student Committee. Enlightened militancy – that way the fridge was regularly full. By the end of the school year, however, we were exhausted, both mentally and physically. Zacarias nevertheless moved into the final, vocational baccalauréat year, and I obtained my Certificate of Technical Education.

Just before the school year ended, we moved again. A friend's mother agreed to put us up in a fairly large but rather insalubrious apartment. In exchange, we undertook to do some work on it for her, but the work was really beyond our capabilities. The walls dripped with damp and the wallpaper was coming away. Our clothes were always clammy. Zacarias was often ill; he had a permanent cold and endless throat infections.

The ever-attentive Fanny brought him medicines – it was out of the question for him to fall seriously ill, because it was the year of the baccalauréat. He had board and lodging during the week; it was just weekends and school holidays that were hard.

Although we had no contact with our mother, we would cross paths with her now and then – Narbonne is a small city. Zacarias and she would ignore one another, but I would say hello – she was my mother, after all. But I tried to make sure that these meetings didn't last too long. As soon as she had a chance, she would bombard me with criticisms of my brother. Zacarias and I hardly ever talked about it, because the whole topic triggered a silent bitterness in him. Despite various problems, Zac got his vocational baccalauréat, and then he passed the entrance exams for the Technical and Commercial Advanced Vocational Diploma in Perpignan, taking the mechanical and electrical engineering option.

His life was finally about to change. He would get a study grant and a room in a university hall of residence. His day-to-day living was taken care of, provided that our mother would agree to give us the necessary papers to get the famous university grant. An illusory wish. So year after year, Zacarias and then I would have to get in touch with a social worker and put together dossiers which had none of the required formalities to present to the Local Education Authority. And luckily they eventually accepted them. It would seem that this kind of situation is very common when parents and grown-up children don't get along.

The following summer, as usual, we broke up stones and repaired roads. In September Zacarias went to Perpignan and took a room in a hall of residence. Fanny was close at hand: she had enrolled in Perpignan on a diploma course in advanced sales and marketing and rented a small apartment in the centre of the city. So they more or less lived together, and the university room was used as a pied-à-terre for friends coming to visit them. For my brother this was the beginning of the student's 'good life'. As for me, I was preparing for the baccalauréat in Narbonne and working in turn as assistant supervisor at the Victor-Hugo school, so during the week there were forty miles between us. But at weekends we usually met up. Zacarias came back regularly from Perpignan. He had also rented a small studio in Narbonne, which he used when Fanny went to see her parents.

At weekends I stayed at the school. Oddly enough, Zacarias never suggested that I should use his place. For a while he seemed to have changed. I felt that that he was less close to me. It must be said that the two years that had just passed had made our relationship more difficult. The arguments we had, usually to do with our precarious situation, had sometimes been quite hard. Instead of drawing us closer together, difficult times had pushed us apart. I was working for the baccalauréat, and I didn't have time to go into things too much. Zacarias spent most of his time with Fanny. He had mid-term exams to prepare for, and the demands of his student life to deal with.

At the end of that year I in turn passed my baccalauréat with distinction and enrolled for the vocational training certificate in Perpignan. I rented a room in a hall of residence. Zac was now living in Fanny's apartment. That academic year – 1989–90 – my brother and I were thus university students. It would be a year dedicated to partying. Every night we ate with this friend or that. We had friends in common, and when Zacarias went to Narbonne he also saw Yves, who had been a secondary-school friend. David, whom he'd also known since that period, was on the same course as he. So in my brother's circle there were old friends to whom he had remained faithful. He also spent time with a Swiss student who was an arms enthusiast.

Every couple of months, we had three days of mid-term exams. So for those three days we did do some work. Even though Zacarias spent his time going out on the town, often without Fanny, he was amazingly faithful to her. And that actually had the effect of attracting the girls even more to him. They would flirt with him in the hopes of landing a prize catch. No such luck!

At the end of the summer of 1990, as I was driving back from the Paris area, I stopped off in Narbonne, to say hello to Jamila. I tooted the horn outside my mother's house. My sister came out from the basement where she had her room, with a girl. Jamila introduced us. The girl was Fouzia, my aunt's daughter, so my cousin. She had come to enrol as a postgraduate student in France. We talked about our respective studies and I offered to take her down to Perpignan. I introduced her to Zacarias and they immediately got on well. Fouzia told us things about our family that we had never heard before. Thanks to her, we got a picture of a harmonious, fulfilled family – one we hadn't known about before. We spent whole evenings asking her about this family member or that. Our family feelings came to life once again, and we felt much more interested in it all. Fouzia's background was totally different from ours. Her family was a close-knit one, and you could feel how much she loved them all. Her parents took an interest in what was happening to her. They phoned her regularly. She told us that they were paying for all their four children's higher education. Naturally enough, Fouzia tried to patch things up between us and our mother. But Zacarias told her how much Aïcha had disappointed him and warned her about Aïcha's fits. Fouzia also talked to us about Moroccan society and the beauty of our country of origin.

In no time Zacarias and I grew very fond of her. We were proud to have such a cousin. We introduced her to all our friends, and they liked her too. Zacarias, who was so discreet about his life with Fanny, introduced them to one another. Zacarias and Fouzia talked a great deal about their respective studies and ambitions. He told her about his import–export project between France and North Africa. But he also talked to her about what she might study. He advised her about the skills that were most sought after in the job market and gave her practical tips for her interviews. We helped her with her administrative paperwork. She enrolled at Marseilles University and when the university term came around we went our different ways. For that year I rarely saw Fouzia, and Zacarias didn't see her at all, although they said hello to each other with me as go-between. At that time my brother felt a brotherly and protective love for his cousin.

Zacarias seemed to be leading a stable life: he was living with the girl he was in love with and he got his certificate without too much trouble. He had finally sorted out his financial problems too. He bought a car: a Ford Fiesta. He had a job as student supervisor in a secondary school in St-Pons, west of Montpellier, a job which, incidentally, he nearly didn't get – the letter from the Education Authority offering him the job went to Aïcha… and never reached Zac. Luckily, when Zac told me that they were really late in answering him, I advised him to get in touch directly with the education authority.

Fanny also got her diploma in sales and marketing. She started studying law and rented a studio apartment. My brother lived with her when he wasn't at the St-Pons school, where he slept three nights a week. He enrolled at Montpellier for a diploma course in economic and social administration.

But, as usual, Zacarias was very demanding: getting his certificate didn't give him equal credits at university. He had to make up diploma course credits, and he didn't like that. What was more, the university system was much less academic than the advanced vocational certificate, for which students had thirty-five hours of classes a week and were very closely supervised by the teachers. University meant freedom: you had to be motivated, because nobody was forced to attend lectures. Beneath his assertive exterior, Zacarias needed to be guided, supported and reassured by his teachers. But at university teachers have very little to do with their students. Supervised projects are over-subscribed, and students have to set up tables in corridors. Zacarias was left to his own devices, and he decided this wasn't right for him.

Some of his friends went on to business school, but that was unthinkable for him because the fees in such establishments were very high: nearly 40,000 francs a year.

Others found jobs. He, too, looked vaguely for work. But he tended to be very quickly discouraged and suspected that each refusal was racially motivated. From that time on, he gradually let himself go. He became more and more unmotivated, and he gave the impression of seeing his student days in a negative light. He had no aim or goal. He was gloomy and weary. Zacarias was sure he had done his very best to get back into an academic curriculum, only to be fettered, at the last minute, by invisible but real chains – the chains of discrimination. Day after day he realized all the more that his diploma wouldn't be enough to open up the doors necessary to work as a sales technician.

He told me that at the national employment agency some of the job ads were colour-coded. Depending on the colour, the job seeker knew whether the company would accept people of foreign origin or not. He also said that the personnel at the employment agency knew very well where it was useless to send a job seeker who was an immigrant... The school year passed like that, a mix of frustration and questioning. The evenings we spent with our friends were full of laughter, but also discussion: it was the period of the Gulf War.

In our part of France, things had become quite tense, to a point where local politicians started to worry that there might be score-settling and confrontation between the born-and-bred French population and the population of North African origin. For a while, the mayor of Perpignan managed to have gun shops closed by means of a prefectural decree. In classes, students quickly split up into two factions: the pro-Americans, who applauded when they saw the bombings going on in Iraq and chanted, 'USA! USA!', and the pro-Arabs, or rather those who were touched by the plight of Iraqi civilians under American bombs. The hall of residence was abuzz with the war in Iraq. The campus was like a meeting place, where all kinds of ethnic groups lived together. A miniature, scaled-down version of the world. There were Swedes and Danes as well as

Christian Lebanese, Palestinians and Syrians. And from the very outset of the Gulf War, the dialogue between the Arabs and the others was a complicated one. No, we didn't go along with Saddam Hussein's regime. But we wholeheartedly condemned the Americans and their allies tossing bombs at civilians. Zacarias wasn't living in the hall of residence, but we hung out with the same friends on campus, and he felt very supportive of the Iraqi people. And then Zacarias with his dark skin, and his girlfriend, with her blonde hair and blue eyes – they both knew what xenophobia was.

One evening I was waiting for the bus to go back to the hall of residence when a guy in a car stopped right beside me. He got out and walked very fast towards me, screaming. He was brandishing a knife. 'Dirty wog. I'm going to get you!' he yelled. Once the initial shock wore off, my reflexes kicked in and that's what saved my skin. In the ensuing fight, I floored him. But at the bus stop there were several people waiting with me. Nobody lifted a finger… The next day, when I told my brother what had happened, I saw his face turn pale and his lips tighten and he didn't say a word.

In that period the things Zacarias and I talked about and discussed with other students inevitably gravitated not only around the issue of the Gulf War but also the situation in Palestine and the civil war in Algeria – decisive events for all Muslims throughout the world. For hours we talked about the legitimacy of the intervention in Iraq. For us, Saddam Hussein had no right invading a country the way he had, but that didn't entitle anybody to massacre the Iraqi people in return. We were very shocked by the 'war show', which was so over-hyped by the media, and in such a one-sided way. The so-called 'surgical' strikes sickened us.

We had mixed feelings: we felt an affinity with those suffering people, not only because they were suffering, but also because they were Muslims. Initially, Saddam Hussein tried to play on those particular feelings. But in no time at all

Arab countries sent in their armies to defend Kuwait. For us Muslims it was a disconcerting war. It wasn't good guys versus bad guys. The truth was more subtle and less a question of right and wrong. That war crystallized feelings against American imperialism, be it political or economic. We had the feeling that the France that sent in troops to fight alongside the Americans against Iraq was not our France.

I think it was at that particular moment that Zacarias started to feel that he belonged to the 'Blacks', whereas people of French extraction were 'Whites'. It was also at that time that he became convinced that the French are racists. That generalization didn't scare him. For him, his friends and my friends, and Fanny too, the few teachers who had helped us were non-racist French. In other words, they were exceptions to the rule. I often tried to tone down his ideas. But every day that he witnessed racism confirmed his painful conviction. The fact was that since the outbreak of the Gulf War attacks against the North African community became more and more frequent, at least in the south of France, where we lived.

And then there was the war in Yugoslavia and Bosnia. The media crudely reported the ethnic cleansing and the massacres of Muslims. Repercussions in the Muslim community ran deep – Yugoslavia was just an hour and a half from Perpignan. And it was Europe. There were Yugoslavian students on campus. We identified very easily with them. Photos of concentration camps with emaciated, sick Muslim prisoners started to be passed around – photos all too reminiscent of the ones of people being shipped off to Nazi concentration camps in our history books. The French government seemed to us to be terribly passive, not to say in cahoots. We felt hurt and humiliated, as much because those people were our brothers as because the other European countries were not reacting. Even the systematic rape of Bosnian women by Serbs didn't seem to disturb very much. And if governments weren't doing anything, wasn't that because the victims in Bosnia were

Muslims? Who can guarantee us that one day the same horror won't be visited upon us French Muslims, and who can guarantee us that other peoples will be any less passive?

The Gulf War, Bosnia, Algeria, Palestine, Afghanistan, Chechnya... Muslims were being persecuted all over the world. That disgusted us. Zacarias wasn't the only one to have this feeling. All Muslims of our age, and even those who were younger were shattered. They felt deeply and personally, in their very flesh, the injustice of which their religious brothers were victim. As they grew older these young Muslims became hypersensitive. They no longer believed in the morality and ethics of rulers. So some of them would be ripe for totalitarian and sectarian ideologies. In my everyday life, I was assailed more often than my brother by brutal racism, and yet he suffered more than I did. Every attack on his older brother put him in an uncontrollable state of inner ferment.

When I told him he was wrong, and that, whatever he might think, the majority of French people weren't racists – that, on the contrary, just a minority of them came across as such – I really felt that not only did I fail to convince him but also that the only ear he lent me was an irritated one. What's more, he would inevitably answer me: 'Abd Samad, you're too nice. You haven't realized that they're all racists and fascists.'

In September 1991 Zacarias needed an administrative certificate from the university to keep his job as supervisor at the secondary school. Buoyed up on his new plan to speak fluent English, he enrolled for the Applied Foreign Languages course at Perpignan. But he would hardly ever set foot in a class there. He got a new job as a supervisor in the Docteur La Croix secondary school in Narbonne. I also found a job as supervisor in Narbonne at the Diderot secondary school.

When that term started we also met Fouzia again. She had had had a good university year and embarked on her degree in pharmacology. By staying at Roche-Grise, Fouzia had been a bit of a witness to our family disputes. She was truly

shocked and her relations with my mother deteriorated a lot.
She felt weary and exhausted. Zacarias and I advised her to
keep her distance. In the end the break came, and Fouzia left
Roche-Grise with the words: 'I don't understand this
situation, it's too much for me, I've finished my studies, and
my resident's permit expires soon, so I'm going back to
Morocco.' Zacarias and I approved of her decision, which we
found quite logical. But before she actually left, we had to find
her somewhere to stay. Zacarias and I had lodgings in the
schools where we worked. So I asked my sister Nadia, who
had an apartment in the centre of Narbonne, to put up our
cousin for ten days. She agreed. Zacarias, Fouzia and I all
spent those few days before Fouzia's departure together. As
soon as our day's work was done, we met up with her. We
went for walks and saw our friends. I still have a few
memories of those days, like that film we saw one Wednesday
afternoon. We'd forgotten that it was children's day, so the
three of us ended up with just a handful of other grown-ups
in a cinema full of kids. The incongruousness of that
particular moment brings back the good feelings there were
between us.

We often went to Perpignan, too, to stay with friends. One
of them was called Xavier, one of my closest friends. We spent
our evenings talking and laughing, and would end the evening
having a really nice time over a meal. The day before Fouzia
left, we met my two sisters and all five of us went for a walk.
We spent that evening with Nadia, over a meal. At the end of
October 1991, Zacarias and I went with Fouzia to Sète where
she would take the boat *Marrakech*. We laughed a lot on the
journey. Those were rare moments of family happiness. It had
been a long time since we siblings had been together.

Talking about our family with Fouzia had aroused in
Zacarias and me a desire to know more about our father. We
wanted to know what had become of him. The latest we'd
heard, he was in Toulouse, so after we'd left Fouzia in Sète we

drove to the pink-brick city. Once there, we got into detective mode. Thanks to the Chamber of Commerce and Local Industry, we got an address. We went to it only to find that he was no longer living there. Then Zacarias and I had the bright idea of contacting the customer service department of the electricity company, with one of us pretending to be our father. We complained that we hadn't had the latest bill and told the employee that there was a problem of addresses, and we wanted to check to see if the one on file was the right one. Bingo! She gave us our father's address, and thanks to her we found him. He was very moved by our visit. We spent a warm evening with him. And naturally enough, he invited us to stay the night. At dawn we were awakened by fearful noise and shouting: 'Police! Police! Open up!' We hardly had time to pull back the covers before five or six cops were in the apartment. They took our father away while we looked on, dumbfounded. Everything happened too fast. The apartment was empty. A deathly silence filled it. We got dressed and set off back to Narbonne. We hardly spoke during the drive, both lost in our thoughts. Why exactly had the police taken him away, that morning in 1991 in Toulouse? I only learned the reason ten years later – it had involved some kind of brawl.

I think that was the last time Zacarias saw our father. I bumped into him again in 1993, in Narbonne, as I left the school at the end of my week as student supervisor. I crossed paths with him at the railway station, with my sister Nadia. He didn't look well; he'd lost a lot of weight and seemed tired.

Zac and I had become very close again. We were once more living in the same city, Narbonne, where we both worked as supervisors, sharing the same friends and evenings together. When Zacarias talked to me about his work, he was critical of the administrative staff. There again, he found them aggressive and stupidly racist. He claimed, for example, that all the supervisors of foreign origin got a worse deal in terms of their working hours. For him, 'racism' had become an obsession, and whether that obsession was legitimate or not it was now wrecking his life.

He spent the rest of the week in Montpellier, where Fanny was still living. And then Fanny gave up her apartment and went back to live with her parents in Narbonne. For those two, as a couple, things were getting more complicated. For Zac, it now seemed crucial to add something 'extra' to his training, which would make a difference in the eyes of a company boss. We talked about it every weekend. I agreed with him, and as we had a female cousin in the United Arab Emirates, we started imagining how our life would be if we started trading with Arab countries, and particularly with Morocco and the Emirates. Zacarias also found out about a Montpellier-based association called Euro-Arabe, which dealt with trade between North Africa and Europe.

Zac thought that the wisest thing, first of all, would be to improve our language skills, so that we could then work abroad. At that time he spoke just broken English, and he still didn't speak Arabic, so he bought textbooks and worked away at English grammar. Every day he forced himself to study on his own, but in the most serious way you could imagine. Despite everything, after a few months my brother realized that he hadn't chosen the best way to go about it: he hadn't found the best method to achieve any kind of fluency. As we talked it over, we eventually agreed that there was nothing like real experience in an English-speaking country. He thought he might find a job as supervisor on the spot, as in France, unless he was eligible for state benefit. Then he would look for a relevant course, even though, in England, you have to pay for higher education. Later on he would have a chance to learn Arabic, and thus be able to work as a sales technician in export between French-speaking countries, English-speaking countries and the Emirates.

In Montpellier, in those days, Zacarias hung out at the cafeteria in the hall of residence. It was an odd kind of place: the students who spent half their day there were mostly foreigners, Moroccans, Algerians, Tunisians, Malians, Senegalese, Syrians and Palestinians. Most of them used the cafeteria like a squat, because they had accommodation problems – especially students in their last two years, because they were given a room only once everyone else had been seen to.

So they would end up five or six in a room, and sleep there on a rotation basis. Those whose turn it wasn't to spend the night in the room had to stay awake, and by day they were too tired to attend classes. In the holidays, the communal kitchens were closed, which only made them feel more out on a limb. They all told us about how degrading it was and the contempt they were treated with. They told us about the uphill battle they were forced to fight just to be able to study. For example, the administrative departments at the prefecture needed their student card in order to issue a resident's permit. And the educational departments needed a resident's permit in order to enrol them. This administrative game-playing went on for months, and students would emerge disgusted and exhausted by this harassment. Most of them ended up saying it would have been better to go to study in the United States or Canada, rather than France.

Added to this precarious student life were money problems. The scholarships handed out by their countries were derisory and their temporary residents' permits bore the rider: 'NOT AUTHORIZED TO WORK'. The most determined and stubborn of them did, nevertheless, manage to attend second-degree courses and embark on doctorships. These students had few hours of classes and they looked for odd jobs to help them make ends meet. Some of those who didn't succeed seemed to me to be cynical and at a loose end. They spent their time talking about the latest international news. Little by little, Zacarias spent hardly any time with born-and-bred French people. His new friends seemed to cultivate an attitude of rebellion. They were forever denigrating politicians and intellectuals – French ones in particular – railing against their blinkered, single-minded thinking. There were probably Muslim Brotherhood members among them. At the university they had a nickname: 'Kid Brothers'.

I was particularly shocked by one of them, a North African. He said he'd received a large grant from his country of origin, yet his arguments were of an extreme violence. What bothered me with him was that he'd been helped by a developing country to pursue his studies, from the baccalauréat to PhD level, and instead of contributing to the development of his country he claimed that it was more to the point to foment revolution there in order to destroy society. One of his sentences still rings in my ears: 'We have to destroy this society so that it can be born again from its ashes.' Once again the reference was Sayyid Qotb.[1]

I think I can say, without fear of contradiction, that it was by rubbing shoulders with these students that Zacarias discovered a dangerous caricature of Islam. Among them he basked in an atmosphere marked by a desire for vengeance. What they had to say about the civil war in Algeria, for example, was extremely ambiguous: 'We don't know what's going on over there. The authorities say it's the Armed Islamic Group (GIA) that is massacring the population, but they don't provide any proof, and it's very likely that they're trying to cover things up.' So it was the same discourse as that of certain leaders of the Islamic Salvation Front (FIS). They also gave me the impression of using certain topics, like war, to their own ends, be it to do with Palestine, Bosnia, or anywhere else. For them, every conflict involving Muslims offered a chance to uphold the highly militant argument of the 'Muslim Brotherhood', probably espousing just causes, but by way of extremist indoctrination and to political and financial ends that would benefit others than themselves.

The more the university year advanced, the less Zacarias turned up for lectures. When he returned to Montpellier, he hung aimlessly about on campus and spent more and more time talking to the 'Kid Brothers'. He also started to develop a specific kind of argument, becoming more and more disillusioned and cynical. When it came to Algeria, he would now say that the political elite was really responsible for the civil war and the massacres. When it came to France, he would argue that the system was rotten and made solely to serve a corrupt, middle class. He would say that for ordinary, humble people, there was just one solution: fend for yourself, or else you'll end up more rotten than the others. I didn't share Zacarias's ideas. I found them excessive and I came to the conclusion quite simply that it was a difficult year for him to live through, because he felt he was failing and he didn't really see how to make things better. He would often repeat pessimistically: 'I studied so that I could manage better, and what's the result? I'm stuck.' Deep down, I thought that that bitterness in him would pass when he finally found his way.

It's also true that not having a family home where you can recharge your batteries didn't help matters. Since he had left our mother's house, he hadn't set foot in it again. We spent our holidays in the lobbies of the hall of residence. When anyone asked him about our mother, Zacarias would inevitably answer: 'She's not my mother. She's my brother's mother.' The only thing he wanted to do was 'leave Narbonne'. At every opportunity he would say: 'All I know is that I've got to leave. I don't know where to, and I don't know when, but I must leave this city.' From that moment on, we talked more and more about the advantages for him of learning English. We even drew up ambitious plans: he would speak English fluently, and he would learn literary Arabic, the Arabic of the Gulf states. Our cousin, who was living in the United Arab Emirates, might possibly be able to help us to start with. While he learned Arabic, I would learn English in turn. And later on we would go into international trading together. When his ideas focused once and for all on England (the United States was too expensive and too far away in case things went wrong), I encouraged him to go there. It seemed to me that, for him, it was also a chance to change environments and company. Naively, I reckoned that it could only do him a world of good to get away from the 'Kid Brothers'. I knew my brother, and I knew that he was not easily influenced – but you never know.

Fanny wasn't at all in agreement with these plans. She had just been taken on as an assistant in a bank, and all she dreamed about was having a quiet life – living with Zacarias somewhere nearby. She wasn't at all keen for him to go away. She encouraged him to go on looking for work. Zac reproached her for not being realistic and not understanding that the colour of his skin was a real drawback when it came to finding a job. The proof: in the region there was great demand for sales technicians in mechanical engineering and electrical engineering, but, he would tell her, when he turned up for a job it was always: 'Too late!' He also told her: 'Do you think it'll be easy for us to find somewhere to live, with my skin colour? You know very well how things are, don't you? I'll have to be a millionaire to get any respect.' All these accumulated frustrations were like so much fertilizer that would make my brother susceptible to an ideology that he would unfortunately come across very readily in England.

At the end of 1991 the pace quickened. Zac sold his Ford Fiesta. He put to one side the money saved on rent since Fanny and he had left their apartment in Montpellier, and he was very careful about how much he spent. As he had board and lodging in Narbonne as a school supervisor, he did manage to put a certain amount of money aside: between 20,000 and 25,000 francs. Together we went to buy a large backpack for his trip. As a safety measure, we bought a money belt for him too. Zacarias set off with all his worldly wealth on his person. He had no idea what he would find where he was going. If somebody robbed him, it would bring his trip to an immediate halt. His intention was to manage to stay at least six months in England. We bought most of the things he needed together. His adventure was a bit mine too, and for the first time he and I were going to be truly parted. He was my little brother – I was at once proud of him, sad and anxious. I was the only person who went to the airport with him. It was a very solemn moment. My brother was setting off on a rendezvous with his destiny…

6

DOWN AND OUT, AND ALONE IN LONDON

Nobody was there was to greet Zacarias in London. When he arrived in England, his first task was to find a place to stay. Before he left, he reckoned he would easily find a quiet and simple youth hostel. But when he phoned me a few days after he arrived, he told me that he'd ended up in St Mark's House – a centre for the homeless. He gave me a phone number where I could reach him, and said that everything was fine and that I shouldn't worry – whatever happened, he would make out. He wanted to get in touch with the Social Services and find ways of getting state benefits. But most important, he wanted to find work fast. At that particular time I phoned him regularly, but our conversations were brief and I only really learned any details about his day-to-day life when he came back to Montpellier more than six months later.

When he landed at Frejorgues Airport in Montpellier, I saw right away that my young brother had changed. He had lost weight and he had grown up. But he had a smile on his face, and he seemed very happy to see me again. And then he betrayed a little sense of pride: he'd managed to last 'over there' for more than six months. But, as he admitted to me not long after, for his first three months his poor English had literally paralysed him. He had spent all that time unable to speak, almost without opening his mouth, so ill at ease did he feel. He said he felt as if he was physically weakened, plunged into a kind of scary loneliness. Not only did he not dare get by in English but he also didn't understand much when people talked to him.

He told me about his day-to-day life in detail, and it seemed very hard to me. The hostel he lived in was rather disreputable. He described his roommates to me with a hollow laugh. One of them behaved completely irrationally, taking dozens of different-coloured pills every day. Another spent the day drinking beer, sprawled on a sofa in the lobby. He was drunk morning to night. Sometimes when the person running the hostel threw him out, he stayed slumped on the steps of the church right beside the hostel. My brother also described his nights. There was a shared dormitory, with several dozen homeless guys, mainly English, sleeping there every night. Zacarias had an iron bed, with his clothes rolled in a bundle under his pillow – everything was up for grabs in that place. And by day, needless to say, there was no question, either, of leaving your personal effects there. Theft and violence were everywhere. We talked at great length about all that underlying insecurity. I felt that he was tense and anxious in an almost palpable way. And then I had an idea: to have a better chance of not being assaulted, you had to be physically imposing. So I suggested that he do some body-building. He liked the idea, even though the cost of it represented for him a real financial investment. As soon as he went back to London, two weeks later, Zacarias joined a body-building club. Now and then he found odd jobs on the side – washing up in a pizzeria, as a warehouse man and the like. Just enough not to fritter away his meagre savings all at once.

After those very difficult beginnings, Zacarias started to feel a bit more at ease in London. He had now been discovering the streets for some months. He finally knew how to get about in that huge city. Every day he forced himself to work on his English, alone with his books in a library. Each week he visited an employment agency. He wasn't looking for a job so much as training. So it was, he told me, that after successfully taking a whole battery of tests, he managed to get into South Bank University, where he would work towards a Master of International Business degree. He reckoned that that university was a branch of Cambridge University. So that would look good on his future curriculum vitae. For at that time my young brother still hadn't lost sight of his goal: to improve his professional training so that he could increase his level of skills. He still had it in mind to get involved with the import–export of *halal* meat – in other words meat that has been slaughtered in accordance with Muslim ritual – with North African countries, for example.

Every time Zacarias came back to France, I felt and saw him becoming harder. He didn't like British society at all, describing to me a country that was grey, rainy and closed. In Great Britain, he said, all ethnic communities were tolerated, but they didn't mix. They lived turned in on themselves, in their neighbourhoods, surrounded by invisible barriers, as if ghettoized. He accused the English of being tolerant only on the surface. What was more, he said: 'After all this time, I've met plenty of people of different nationalities, but the only ones I don't know at all are the English.' Even at the university, contact with English students was very superficial. He said he'd met more British students on the Perpignan and Montpellier campuses.

I tried to understand him a bit better every time he came back to France. When he left, Zacarias experienced a real psychological shock. The contrast both bruised and hardened him – the difference between the life he had previously lived, with Fanny, his friends, his brother, in his own country, and his present-day life, which was that of an immigrant in Britain, on his own, and not speaking the language. But he rightly considered that he had fulfilled a personal challenge by standing his ground. That victory gave him more confidence in himself and somehow gave him more weight. That was also what would attract Xavier and another friend, Hartium to him. Luckily for Zac, he managed to move out of the homeless hostel. He told me he had got a scholarship, the equivalent of 150,000 francs, to pay for his year at the university and for lodgings, a fully furnished, two-room flat in the centre of London. I only learned later that the address he gave me was in one of the more elegant parts of town, Nevern Square, in Earl's Court.

Even today I still don't know if he really lived in that famous university flat that he described to me, or whether he actually lived in a flat that was as luxurious as the neighbourhood. A flat that he certainly couldn't have afforded on his own, anyway. All I know is that some student midwives lived there. Zacarias also talked to me about a part of London where he often went, a neighbourhood frequented by foreigners – mainly Algerians and Moroccans. When we talked about the civil war in Algeria, we didn't have the same opinions. I knew, through the media, that members of the Islamic Salvation Front and the Armed Islamic Groups were based in London and that they were at liberty to express their hatred, in the streets and mosques. I also knew perfectly well that my brother had no religious background. So I decided it was time to send him, in England, an explanatory pamphlet about the Wahhabis which the At-Tawba Mosque in Montpellier had published. That was a mistake, as I would realize later.

In 1993 and 1994 Zacarias came back to France about every four months, mainly to see Fanny. Meanwhile, I met my future father-in-law and asked him for Fouzia's hand in marriage. Then we got married. It was a small but very happy wedding. We showed Zacarias the photos. He congratulated us but said he was sorry we hadn't told him. He would have come over for it. Knowing his financial situation, that was precisely what we wanted to avoid.

Every time Zacarias came back to France, he stayed with us. He never talked to us about religion. Yet it was in that same period that I started to practise Islam. He could have shown a dash of curiosity, but he didn't. On the contrary, even, he treated my religious practice somewhat mockingly. It's true that, as a novice and not reading Arabic, I had to write the words to be said during prayers in large letters on a sheet of paper. In 1994 I suggested that he come with me to Friday prayers at the mosque. He refused, preferring to go into town. Today, I can analyse his reaction in a new light. At that particular moment, he probably hadn't yet met the people who would become his 'gurus'. Or at least he hadn't yet been truly recruited.

That same year, on another occasion, I tried to find a way of entertaining him. It so happened that there was the end-of-year school party at the mosque. To honour and reward the children, the Association of Islamic Welfare Projects in France (APBIF) organized that party every year. The children put on cultural shows and recited historical events. A school party, in a word, though it did perhaps have one distinctive feature, which was its singing group. A dozen children sang Arab–Andalusian Sufi chants. They were a roaring success. Zacarias came with me as far as the entrance to the hall but refused to go in. He told me it didn't interest him and that it was all just 'innovation'.[1] He said he was interested only in the Koran and the Sunna.[2] The imam arrived to preside over the party, and I took advantage of this to introduce my brother to him. A discussion ensued. I asked the imam to tell my brother how you learn the science of religion. Zacarias cut me off and snapped: 'Personally, all I need is the Koran and the Sunna to learn about religion, I'm quite capable of getting hold of books and studying them on my own. ' And the imam replied: 'Then if you are prepared to spend ten years finding out how to do your minor ablutions in the Sunna or the Koran, good luck!'

A strange discussion: can you become a doctor because

you have learned medicine all on your own without any teachers, just from books? Who would go and be operated on by somebody who claims they've learned about surgery on their own in libraries? On almost all of his visits, Zacarias borrowed my car to go to Narbonne and see Jamila. While she was living with my mother, they both made sure that he never met with her. When he arrived at the house, he honked the horn from a distance, and Jamila would come straight out. Things were getting difficult with Fanny. The last time I saw them together was in 1993 in Montpellier; they were spending the weekend in a cottage they had rented. Fanny was still working at the bank. She wanted to set up home and live with my brother. She wanted to have a family, and a normal life. She probably asked him to come back to France, but Zacarias's goal was to get rich. 'I must keep moving on, and earn money,' he would often repeat. He refused to give up the possibility of a better future, just to please Fanny.

He, in turn, asked her to go to England. But Fanny knew that life was hard over there. What would be the point in her following him, just to have a tough time? They were both at a dead end, and so was their love for each other, which had endured for ten years. Zacarias, in turn, was deeply wounded by her refusal to follow him. He who out of respect never talked about her to me, told me at that particular time: 'She's a middle-class girl. All she thinks about is her creature comforts and herself. She doesn't really love me.' There was a tone of scorn and pain in his voice. He was terribly disappointed. That period marked the end of their love affair. Zacarias is very sentimental, all or nothing. And his deception was on a par with his commitment. He would have moved mountains for Fanny. He felt she wasn't ready. But was it really necessary to move mountains?

From that particular moment, things moved fast. When Zacarias came back the following year, I found him quite different. Usually, whenever we met up again, we talked very freely and warmly about things. Just like two brothers who have shared memories, moments of great happiness and moments of real pain from the year dot. This time I suddenly realized how powerless I was. I was simply unable to engage him in any dialogue. My brother was there, right next to me, and yet I felt he was far, far away. As if he wasn't there at all. He answered my questions about his daily life rather perfunctorily. Fouzia and I therefore thought that maybe he needed some privacy, to be alone and that he didn't dare tell us that. So we let him stay in our little apartment, on his own, and we stayed in my supervisor's room at the school. Zacarias also had use of our car and we left the fridge filled for him.

In the evenings my wife would prepare him tasty little dishes. Fouzia is a great cook. However, not only did this not cheer him up but he was never satisfied. He complained. Fouzia was taken aback by this change in his attitude towards her. Up until then, he'd always shown great affection for her; he had always been courteous and attentive. At the end of 1992, on his first trip back from England, the three of us had had great times laughing and dreaming about the future. Up until 1994, Zacarias and Fouzia had always had very deep conversations. They talked about their respective studies and their possible job prospects. At that time Fouzia was working towards her school teaching qualification in biology, and Zacarias would encourage her to work even harder and, because she was gifted, to take her studies as far as she possibly could. But now his argument had radically altered. He no longer seemed in favour of studying, at least not for women. He would say over and over to Fouzia: 'Studies aren't important for women. You'd be better off staying at home.'

One night, when the three of us were watching a film on TV, in which a woman was hit by her husband, Zacarias said ironically: 'Serves her right. That's what women need.' Fouzia and I were aghast. My brother, an undeniably intelligent young man, who was usually open, ready to talk about things, and interested in other people, was turning more and more in on himself. And when he did say something, it was to make aggressive remarks and uphold diehard ideas. He could spend a whole day without talking, and he never went out of the house. He stayed slumped in an armchair, and if you went on at him and asked him questions, he would answer with a simple 'yes' or just a 'no'. Needless to say, his behaviour worried me. I thought he had lost his bearings and that a serious depression was imminent. I asked him: 'Are you sure things are OK? Can I do something for you? Anyway, you know you can count on me.' But he would systematically reply: 'No, it's nothing, I'm tired. You know I've been having a hard time for months…' I tried to get him to change his ideas. To show him that it was important to me, that I loved him, that he was my younger brother and that he could rely on my help. My wife and I tried to reassure him. But I felt helpless. He'd become a stranger. The year was 1995. Zacarias went back to London where, so he said, he was going to get his MBS degree.

The next time I saw him was in a photo, a few days after September 11th, 2001.

In Montpellier, a few weeks after those tragic events, I met a teacher friend, a born-and-bred French man who had converted to Islam and had been living in Britain for the past fifteen years. He was very informed about extremist movements. When we met we had a really interesting discussion about the situation in Britain. In his opinion, although the great majority of British Muslims are Sunnites and essentially Hanafites, a very large number of sects and extremist organizations are rife in Britain. Until September 11th 2001 the British government seemed hardly bothered, and it was only when serious incidents occurred, like the attempted attack in Yemen organized by Abu Hamza, that it seemed to take notice and get agitated. The allowances payable to Omar Bakri – the former director of Hizb Attahrir (the Party of Liberation) in England, then founder of the Al-Muhajiroun (the Immigrants Movement) – were suddenly and brutally cut off, as a result of the arguments of a Member of Parliament who found it scandalous that a man openly preaching the destruction of the British state could be the beneficiary of such institutional financial support. My friend told me that Wahhabi movements in England are part of a whole host of diverse organizations, usually hostile to one another, essentially devoted to recruiting members from the Muslim youth of the country and displaying very different attitudes towards their host country. Until September 11th the rule that everybody seemed to abide by was 'no attacks in Great Britain' – because they had a completely free hand within the Muslim and the Caribbean community.

In a small neighbourhood he knows, lived in mainly by Muslims, there is a large mosque run by a Wahhabi movement from the Indian subcontinent, called the Ahl-e Hadith (the people of the Hadith). There is also a bookshop, a prayer centre, a church turned into a primary school and a training school for adults belonging to another Wahhabi movement – the so-called Salafites – officially in line with the doctrine of the Saudi state. My friend told me how this particularly active movement apparently benefited from huge financial backing, because its small membership would certainly not enable it to have so many buildings and centres, or recruit so many people from the Caribbean.

Until recently, in his view, each little movement ran a certain number of centres quite openly and freely, in front of the very eyes of the English authorities. The distinctive feature of the Wahhabi movement is its plentiful funds. In other respects it has the same brutal and contemptuous attitude towards the local Muslim population. Another feature of this movement in England is that it seems to be a perfect reflection of the religious divisions and conflicts existing in

Saudi Arabia. Wahhabi groups exist which, up until September 11th, could openly enlist young people and send them to Afghanistan, Kashmir and Chechnya, raise funds and distribute their propaganda outside mosques and in certain Muslim institutions. These groups do not support the present Saudi government, even though their religious references (Ahmad ibn Taymiyya, Muhammad ibn 'Abd al-Wahhab, Ibn Al-Qayyim Al-Jawziyya, etc.) are the same as those of these so-called Salafites and other Ahl-e Hadith-like groups. He told me that the Salafites officially declare themselves to be against all forms of terrorism and distribute a pamphlet written by one of their current leaders, Ibn Baz, in which he denounces the attacks in Saudi Arabia organized by bin Laden. Their politics seem to be in keeping with those of the Saudi Ministry of Religious Affairs.

He actually reckons that the fact that bin Laden would be 'king' instead of the current king represents the only real stumbling block. This is why some support violent actions while others don't. In any event, these brother enemies teach their members that they are the only believers on earth, and that Muslims are a bunch of superstitious and idolatrous ignoramuses. Their attitude within the community is notorious for its intolerance, and their verbal and physical abuse of anybody who stands up to them is a well-known public fact. My friend had first-hand experience of it. He also reckons that this movement, like many other groups, but in a more blatant way than them, has a very powerful presence not only in colleges, where many young people aged between sixteen and eighteen prepare for their A-levels, but also in universities. In these establishments, the Wahhabis set up so-called 'Islamic Societies' and Koran and Sunna Societies, which organize activities and courses and give assistance to those they hope to recruit. When they themselves do not found a 'society', they work their way into existing societies until they gain control of them, and at that point they assume absolute power over them and use them as a branch of their movement within the establishment. Their preachers, and theirs only, come to indoctrinate young audiences who are uninformed and frustrated by the pitiful state of their local and international community. These brainwashing sessions are called 'lectures' or talks. According to my friend, to wrest control of an association from this movement you have to fight tooth and nail against an administration which has no idea about what is going on and which has its own reasons for turning a blind eye. A student or a young foreigner who goes to England, or a young person with immigrant parents, finds a markedly Sunnite community, where most of the teachers and religious dignitaries speak only Urdu, Arabic or Bengali. Even the children of Pakistani parents have a very poor knowledge of the language of their ancestors, and even less so when this language is at the high level required by religious instruction. In fact the only religious literature in English that you find in any quantity is Wahhabi. Wahhabis have lots of bookshops. They hand out large numbers of pamphlets and booklets in the street and in markets, and even in the main shopping streets in city centres, and in addition bookshops which do not belong to them still sell their books.

In his eyes, there is a real generation gap in England within the Muslim community, with, on the one hand, parents and grandparents who are too ignorant to quench young people's thirst for knowledge, and religious people who do not really have enough language to communicate effectively with them; and, on the other hand, a whole host of preachers and writers with a very solid foothold in colleges and universities, who are often their age or thereabouts. 'I didn't find out much about the Finsbury Park Mosque or Abu Qatada that hasn't been on English TV: it's outside my area and I don't have any personal contact with those people', he told me. 'One day, talking about the young people arrested in Yemen after being sent there by Abu Hamza, one of my students told me that he reckoned he'd had a narrow escape because he and his friends were well on the way to becoming future Abu Hamza volunteers. In the end, because they started to learn about religion with a Sunnite teacher, they moved away from that group and thus got out of the grips of that harmful influence,' he told me.

This friend gave me three examples of the sort of thing that went on, on a regular basis, in the Muslim community in London up until September 11th. He also went to a lecture at an Islamic Circle given by a recruiting agent from one of the organizations training people in Afghanistan. This circle often invited all kinds of people to hear their ideas, sometimes even non-Muslims were invited, such as people in the hierarchy of the Catholic Church. The young man presenting this lecture to a dozen or so people (mainly young people, twenty-something) spoke with deference about Sheik Omar Abderrahman, imprisoned by the Americans in the wake of the first attack on the World Trade Center, and made much of the humiliating and degrading treatment which the authorities had put him through. He then went over a litany of war facts, repeatedly making reference to the victories of the Afghan resistance during the Russian occupation, and little by little he worked the young people up into a state of great agitation. At the end of the lecture, my friend picked out one or two in the audience who were ready to follow this guy. The speaker boasted about the power of his organization (but I don't recall him mentioning the name) and the fact that nobody seemed able to touch them.

The second example is of a man who calls himself Sheik Feisal, who, shortly after September 11th, was arrested as a result of emergency measures taken by the British government. Prior to that, this man, of Jamaican extraction, who had studied at Riyadh University in Saudi Arabia, had travelled the length and breadth of England preaching the jihad with great vigour. He was well known for his extremely uncompromising attitude. Although he had never been involved in the jihad himself, his message everywhere was that everyone should head for the front, and anyone who didn't was a heathen. My friend told me that when a young woman said to him that her husband did not wish to leave and preferred to wage the jihad by teaching Islam, Feisal told her that her husband had become an apostate and that as a result their marriage was null and void. The young woman left her husband after hearing this. A former follower of this Abdullah Feisal left him because he had ended up becoming bored by his continual excommunications, and because, in his eyes, this agitator thought he was the only Muslim on earth, because anybody who disagreed with him over the tiniest little thing was treated like a renegade.

The third and very recent example was related to my friend by a Muslim colleague. At a lunch, he complained about the suffering that one of his cousins was in the process of inflicting on his immediate family and on all his other relatives in general. His cousin had gone to the centre of the so-called Salafites, who had managed to persuade him that their opinions were valid. Seeing that his bonds with his family might get in the way, they told him not to worry about his wife. According to them, anyone not following them is an idolater, whose marriage with one of their members has no validity. They were prepared to provide him with a wife. Their women are usually easy to identify because they are clad in a long black cloak which covers them from head to foot, and they also wear a veil over their face and usually black gloves. Back home, the young man started to lay into the Sunnite beliefs and traditions of his family. When his family became worried over the consequences for his marriage, he told them that his new friends had promised to find him another wife. This teacher was truly shocked – his cousin's family was totally distraught and at a loss.

According to my friend, this sort of situation is not uncommon. It is well known that when a member of a family starts to come under the influence of these Wahhabis, their fanaticism causes their relatives colossal problems, because they don't accept any half-measures. You're either totally with them or totally against them. From what he had managed to gather, most of the young people who fall into the clutches of these Wahhabi sects end up leaving them either sickened or exhausted. After all, it's not easy to belong to a small group which is hated and feared by the community, and which, in addition, hardly lets you have any private life and keeps tabs on every little thing you say. But the scars live on, and much of the damage done is irreparable. The problem is that in the meantime, during their period with these extremists, they are ready to do quite literally anything. If the group is a legalist one, they keep quiet about local laws and the powers that be. If it's not, they do anything they think necessary.

Another problem that afflicts those who spend time with them is their attitude towards women and relations between the two sexes. My friend has told me that, according to a woman teaching Islamic studies at a college, two young Wahhabis who had signed up for one of her courses demanded to have two separate lessons, one for the boys and another for the girls. She sent them packing, but she often has problems with Wahhabis taking her classes. Another female colleague, who ventured into one of their bookshops to look for a book which she wanted to use for her teaching, told him that she had been shocked at how fiercely they had tried to ignore her, and with what ill will they'd ended up serving her. I don't know if she realizes that we other Muslims have to live all the time with these people – as neighbours or as relatives.

And by way of conclusion he said:

> In fact, little of consequence has changed since September 11th. Life for Muslims has become much trickier because of the open hostility shown by non-Muslims after the attacks on the World Trade Center. Still, only those extremists

who preached violence and had obvious links
with al-Qaeda are overtly hassled. As for all the
Wahhabi groups who officially reject terrorism,
they are still rife and enjoying impunity in our
community with funding that seems bottom-
less. Meanwhile, Sunnite Muslims have to
travel the country, going from mosque to
mosque, just to scrape together every penny to
have enough money to build a neighbourhood
mosque… If they're in a hurry, then they have
to turn to Saudi Arabia for funding, which is
easily had, but at a price – Wahhabi preachers
and books included.

The attitude of the authorities and
organizations (police, education, etc.) is exactly
the same as that of the British government with
regard to Saudi Arabia. In private, they
acknowledge that they are backward, misogy-
nistic and fanatical. But officially they defend
them, support them and claim that they are not
in a position to meddle in their affairs, turn a
blind eye to their excesses, heave a sigh and
carry on as ever before. They know that the
terrorists' ideology is exactly the same as the
ideology of the so-called Salafites and their kin;
they know too that their differences actually
have to do with their allegiance to the Saudi
religious authorities and government (two
problems that are at once separate and
connected). Meanwhile, for most young people
coming from an immigrant background,
converts and foreign students, the first message
with Islamic connotations which they pick up
in a language they speak, through all the most
modern media (the Internet is full of their

sites), and by way of a whole host of preachers, lecturers and writers, is the message of Wahhabism and other extremist groups.

I find the lack of consideration towards women on the part of Wahhabite followers extremely shocking and scandalous. But when you become acquainted with the concepts and claimed fatwas spread about by their leaders, you get a better idea of the roots of this scourge. Here is an example: with regard to women working, the Kuwaiti newspaper *Al-Qabas* of Friday 14 June 1996 published a fatwa by Ibn Baz, former Mufti of Saudi Arabia: '...the call for women to go forth and take part in areas which have to do with men is a very serious act for Muslim society. One of the major effects of this is the mixing of sexes which is regarded as one of the greatest forms of fornication which massacre society and destroy its values.'

Another Wahhabi leader, Al Outhaymine, observes on the matter of women driving cars:

Of course the driving of cars by women encompasses many misdeeds. Among these misdeeds is the fact that the woman driving must uncover her face. Now, the face is an element of attraction which is particularly sought after by men's eyes. In fact, a woman is only considered beautiful or ugly in an absolute sense on the basis of her face. In other words, when one says of a woman that she is beautiful or ugly, the mind thinks only of the face, but when one focuses on other elements one then says that she has beautiful hands, beautiful hair, beautiful feet. So it is indeed the face which is the focus when one attributes beauty to a person. Some people may say that it is possible for a woman to drive without unveiling her face. She could veil the lower part of her face and wear dark glasses. The answer to this is that it is contrary to the customs of women to drive cars. Ask those who have observed them in other countries. Even if we admit that it is possible to apply this solution at the outset, it will not last very long but will swiftly evolve towards the same situation for women as in other countries.

As in other areas, the initial regression is relatively benign. However, it soon gathers momentum and degenerates rapidly. Among the misdemeanours implicit in the driving of cars by women, there is the disappearance of propriety... Because those who enjoy driving cars find therein a certain pleasure, and this is why you find them driving here and there for no good reason and quite simply because they derive pleasure therefrom. Among the various misdemeanours, there is also the fact that the woman becomes free. She goes for what she wants, when she wants and where she wants in order to have what she wants, because she is alone in her car. She goes out when she wants and at any hour she wants of the day or night, and may perhaps stay out until a late hour of the night. And if people nowadays suffer from this when it comes to young men, what then is the situation with young women? Wherever she wishes, right or left, she may travel the length and breadth of the country and even possibly go abroad. Among further misdemeanours there is the fact that this is a cause of women's rebellion against their family and against their husbands. For the slightest annoyance, she leaves her home and goes off in her car, to somewhere where she may breathe and find relief – this also occurs with certain young men although they have a greater capacity to put up with things than women. Among the misdemeanours, again, there is also the fact that this is a cause of debauchery in many situations: when stopped at road signs, in petrol stations, at checkpoints or by traffic officers when investigating a crime or an accident or even when they stop to put air in their tyres or indeed if they have a breakdown on the road, they will then need help. So what will become of them then? Perhaps a woman will come upon a perverted man who will make advances to her and take advantage of her honour in exchange for helping her out of her difficulty. Especially if her need for help reaches a certain degree of urgency. Among the misdemeanours there is also the rise of accidents, for women by their nature are less confident, less objective and have lesser capacities than men. So if the woman is assailed by a danger, she will be incapable of acting. Among the misdemeanours there is also the fact that this causes overwork because of the costs. It is a fact that, by her very nature, a woman is fond of the superfluous in anything to do with clothing. Do you not see how attached women are to what they wear? As soon as a new fashion emerges, women make a dash to have it even if it is uglier than what she has already. Do you not see how the walls of her bedroom are

decorated? So by deduction, this same spend-
thrift desire will be more pronounced for the
car, for every time a new model comes out the
woman will abandon the old car for the new.[3]

All this, needless to say, is sheer rambling, falsification and
falsehood. There is nothing in the religious writings to
support this kind of assertion. What's more, this claimed
fatwa is based merely on personal statements and has no
basis in Muslim law. Religion is not a matter of personal
opinion. In effect, it is just another example which helps us to
see the true face of the Wahhabite ideology.

7

THE BRAINWASHING OF ZACARIAS

In the summer of 1996 my wife and I decided to have a holiday in Morocco. I knew Zacarias would probably come to France, as he did every summer, but I didn't know exactly when. I hadn't had a whisper out of him for a year.

I hadn't been to Morocco for nineteen years. I was eager to see the other members of my family and look at their faces again. The last time we'd spent time together, I was ten. My grandmother, my aunt, my uncles and cousins... what had become of them? It's true that I knew only two uncles, six female cousins and an aunt, but I was very fond of all of them, and they of me too. But there were many more I'd only talked to on the phone. Seeing them in Morocco would be like putting faces to voices. The mere thought of meeting them all filled me with joy. I got ready for our journey well ahead of time, like an impatient child waiting for his birthday. I gave my car a service. And suddenly it was time to set off. We stopped by to say goodbye to all our friends. I called the family to tell them we were on our way.

We left early one evening, but before long the car started playing up. The fan belt was up to its old tricks, but rather than turn around and head back to Montpellier, which would have delayed us, we decided to wait until the engine had cooled. So we drove down through Spain with the car in a

pitiful state. I didn't stop to sleep and covered nearly a
thousand miles in one go. When we got to Algeciras, I called
the family to let them know we were OK and we took the
ferry across. I was exhausted but in good spirits. The crossing
took only two hours, but it seemed to last for ever. Tangier
finally loomed on the horizon. Our feelings were running
strong. After an absence of nineteen years, I was looking at
Morocco once more, land of my forefathers. There before my
eyes lay the dazzling contrast of white houses and the deep
blue of the Mediterranean. I was beside myself with joy. We
disembarked in Tangier. Fouzia's father, my uncle – and now
my father-in-law too – was there to meet us. A moving
gesture: he'd driven two hundred miles to welcome us.

I had an important appointment as soon as we landed:
Sheik Abdel Aziz ibn As-Siddiq Al-Ghoumari, a highly
renowned Sunni theological scholar and author of many
books about the Prophetic tradition, jurisprudence based on
religious law and Sufi teachings, was to receive us at his
home. His brother, Sheik Abdallâh, enjoyed even greater
renown, and his books were more focused on warning readers
against Wahhabism. Their father had the status of
'jurisconsult[1] in Islam'. The imam at the At-Tawba Mosque in
Montpellier, where I'd been taking courses in theology for a
couple of years, had recommended that I seek counsel from
him.

Sheik As-Siddiq received us most warmly in his home in
the medina. He ushered us into his large living-room, which
must have measured a good twenty-five by thirty feet. Bench
seats along the walls and low carved wooden tables conveyed
all the beauty of Moroccan craftsmanship. The ceiling was
made of finely carved plaster, with a magnificent chandelier
in the middle. It was very attractive. We talked in quiet tones
about the instruction I was receiving, and he encouraged me
to carry on along that path. After an hour I changed tack. I'd
also come to see him about my brother, because I was

worried. Just before leaving for Morocco, I'd seen my sister Jamila, who had let me in on a secret: the year before, Zacarias had been to see her and had said: 'Abd Samad and Fouzia are doing *tawassul*, they're heathens. Be on your guard with them, but whatever else happens don't say anything to them.'

Tawassul for Sunni Muslims is an invocational formula whereby a person asks Allah to grant him a favour or help him to avoid a problem by citing the name of a prophet or saint in honour of the person cited. For example: 'I ask Allah, through the Prophet Muhammad to grant me piety.' The Wahhabis reckon that this is akin to idolatry for, in their book, 'no one may use an intermediary to address Allah'. Yet it is the Prophet himself who taught a non-seeing man to say: 'Oh, Allah, I beseech Thee and turn to Thee through our Prophet Muhammad, the Prophet of mercy. Oh, Muhammad, I turn through Thee to my Lord so that my need may be filled. Oh, Allah, accept his intercession in my favour and my intercession in favour of my own person.' And when the leg of the great companion Abdallah ibn 'Oumar was paralysed, he called out, 'Oh, Muhammad!', although the Prophet was deceased, and straightaway he regained the use of his leg by the will of Allah.

But Wahhabis are extremists, and their rejection of the *tawassul* is a pretext for declaring that all Muslims in the world are heathens and idolaters who must be dealt with. When Jamila told me what my brother had said, I was taken aback. It made me feel sick, and I ended up in the A&E department with shooting pains in my stomach: on the one hand, because his argument instantly reminded me of Wahhabi beliefs, and I'd never suspected that my bright, well-educated brother, with his stalwart character, could possibly be taken in by that ideology; on the other hand, because he had insisted that Jamila say nothing about it – a sign that he was wary of me.

And I had seen and understood nothing for all those days spent with him, maybe all those years. Now, all the oddness of his behaviour came flooding back into my mind. Now, I could make a different analysis of his silences, and his sadness, and what I took to be depression. Maybe he was quite simply very ill at ease with Fouzia and me because he regarded us as heathens? And to think that he didn't seem to be interested in religion. I spent hours and hours thinking about it and going over the tiniest details about him on his visits to France. I had trouble believing that the abyss I was getting a glimpse of was real. But I had to be clear in my mind about it. So that's why I asked for advice from Sheik As-Siddiq, an authority on the subject.

I duly told the sheik what Jamila had told me. He listened to me very attentively in silence. When I'd finished speaking, the sheik said: 'Your brother is a Wahhabi. And the Wahhabis are dangerous. You must be on your guard, and beware of the Wahhabi creed.' For another whole hour the sheik told me all about Wahhabis. And he stressed that they were a violent people. When we left his house, I knew that my brother belonged to a dangerous group. The sheik's final word of advice still rings in my ears: 'Stay away from the Wahhabis.'

When we were finally with our family, I told them about my conversation with Sheik As-Siddiq. Certain people then told me that earlier that year my brother had made a whirlwind visit to Morocco, that his behaviour was more than strange, and that nobody understood what was going on. Everything for him was forbidden (*haram*), but he was contradicting himself. So he would forbid others to smoke and yet he would go to a corner of the building to smoke cigarettes. Everywhere Zacarias went in Morocco he left a disconcerting impression that was hard to describe. People told me that they felt uncomfortable with him. Now I understand why.

During my visit to Morocco I saw my grandmother again

– a very touching reunion. She took me by the hand and said: 'Come, I will give you a lesson in religion. I saw your brother a few months ago. He was behaving strangely and saying untrue things about religion. So I want you to pay attention. You must learn the Muslim religion in the four Sunnite schools of jurisprudence. These four schools are the Malikite, Chafiite, Hanafite and Hanbalite. Here in Morocco we follow the Malikite school. Anyone who does not recognize the four traditional schools and yet claims to teach religion is a liar. Be very careful. Watch out also for those who are called 'Ikhwan muslimin'[2] for they more deserve the name 'Ikhwan moujrimin'.[3] They are people who assassinate and do abominable things in the name of Islam. No, my son, Islam has never said to do what they are doing. Remember, my son: moderation and the happy medium make things more beautiful.'

There were more surprises in store for Fouzia and me. A few weeks later we returned to France and we went back to Narbonne to see Jamila. And this time she told us that Zacarias had just been staying with her for a few days. To start with she had been very taken aback by how he looked. Zacarias wore a full beard and had a shaven head. He was wearing trousers which came halfway down his calves. But it was above all his behaviour that shocked her. One morning, she told us, she put on quite a long, short-sleeved dress and got ready to go shopping. But Zacarias snapped at her: 'You're not going to go out looking like a whore!' Jamila froze. She spun round and went to him and said evenly: 'What do you mean talking to your sister like that? What's the matter with you? What's up?' Zacarias then mumbled a few incomprehensible words and went to his room. A few moments later he came back out crying and collapsed on the sofa asking her to forgive him. Jamila didn't understand a thing, but she saw that he was suffering. He was her kid brother and she comforted him.

When she told me all that, I realized that my brother was in a bad way. He seemed to be going through a most painful internal struggle. He seemed to be prey to a deep-seated moral torment. Jamila also told me that Zacarias had left her some religious books and urged her to read them. He told her that he would be calling her and giving her advice over the phone. And in fact he did call her a few weeks later. He flew into a rage when she admitted that she hadn't read the books. My sister gave me those books. Needless to say, they were books written by Wahhabis.

But that wasn't all. Zacarias also got up to his tricks in the Narbonne mosque. He went to the Friday sermon, when the mosque was full and there were lots of young people. My brother addressed them. 'I'm going to give you a lesson,' he said to them. The congregation was surprised but polite, and let him speak. And Zacarias started to explain the Wahhabi creed to them. But those particular young folk, who had a religious education, rejected his nonsense. The discussion became heated. Just when Zacarias was reciting alleged verses of the Koran in French, the imam walked into the mosque. He listened to my brother for a few seconds and then asked him: 'Can you speak Arabic?' Zacarias answered him: 'No.' 'So how do you know that what you are saying is the true meaning of what is said in the Koran? You haven't been able to check it in the Book, because it is revealed in Arabic. What's more, the real Muslim belief consists in believing that everything that exists is created by Allah. Allah is neither a body, nor an image, nor a colour, nor a light, nor a statue, for all those are created by Allah. It is not possible to believe that Allah is in one place. He is not in one place. How would it be possible for the Creator to be in one place? Allah existed before the creation of places. It is Allah who created places. He has no need for them. It is impossible to compare Allah with His creatures and if He were not thus, Allah would be like creatures and thus subject to the same effects which they undergo, such as weakness and death. For example, if two beings look alike, then why call one creator and the other creature, because they are similar? So the Creator does not resemble what He creates. What is peculiar to creatures in terms of characteristics cannot be attributed to the Creator. He is not affected by imagination and He is not grasped by reason. He does not limit himself in our mind. He does not take shape in the imagination. The imagination cannot give Him an image, and reason gives Him not a justification; He is beyond it. In the Koran, Allah says of Himself, "Nothing resembles Him and it is He who hears and sees" (Verse 11 of Achoura sura). An extraordinary saint, Dhu I-Nun al-Misri, said: "Whatever you imagine in your mind, Allah is different."' Zacarias lost his temper. He got to his feet and tried to hit the imam. The young people intervened and threw him out. Zacarias walked off hurling insults at them and calling them *kouffar* – heathens.

From that moment on there were no two ways about it: my brother had been recruited by a sectarian group. But what is a sectarian group? The definition of the word in *Webster's International Dictionary*, for example, is simple: a 'sectarian' person is 'one characterized by a narrow and bigoted adherence to a sect'. The reality is more complicated and more subtle. If we put forward the hypothesis that the Wahhabi sect to which Zacarias belongs is connected to the al-Qaeda organization, it is important to imagine how this organization functions. It is a huge tentacular creature. At the very top there is its head, but it has countless tentacles and each one of its arms is capable of moving independently of the others, even if it is linked to the head. Why was Zacarias attracted by this organization?

In 1996, as we have seen, Zacarias told my sister that my wife and I, together with our entire family, were heathens. He caused a scandal in the Narbonne mosque. I realized, but only at that particular moment, that he had 'passed to the other side'. How and with whom? The names Abu Qatada and Abu Hamza recur repeatedly whenever one discusses the movements of European al-Qaeda members in Great Britain.

Contrary to what the West has long thought, the al-Qaeda organization is highly structured. The people running this organization have really put a lot of thought into ways of spreading their ideology among young people, so that they become suitable fodder to be used for the preparation and execution of their actions. These young people first have to be recruited. I think they go about this in Great Britain in the same way they do elsewhere in Europe, in France and in Germany. The only difference is that, up until September 11th 2001, recruiters in Great Britain didn't even have to hide. In France they have to be a bit more discreet. This is not necessarily any more reassuring...

The 'recruiters' invariably proceed in the same way. First of all, they pick out young people who have been estranged from their families, whether this has been imposed or chosen. These young people, with no adult to guide them, are thus cut off from the strong moral anchors that are their father, mother, brothers and sisters, and even friends. The extremely chaotic personal and family history of Zacarias reveals someone deprived of these anchors. I was his only safeguard. But in London he was far away from me. In the early stages of what can only be called an exile, we talked very often on the phone and he returned regularly to France. On those visits he talked to us about his daily life. Then he changed. Gradually, he became more aloof. He stopped telling me details about his life, he became taciturn. He had always been discreet, but now he became secretive. He no longer told me who he was meeting, or how he spent his days, and even less about what exactly he lived off. A state of non-communication developed.

He also changed physically. His features grew hardened. As we have seen, I misinterpreted all these changes. First and foremost I put them down to the problems he might be having living abroad. I didn't want to dramatize the situation, so I stuck strictly to my role as elder brother – accommodating, warm and patient. And I got it all wrong: Zacarias was in the process of ripping up his last roots. Those Wahhabi and Qotbist gurus try to cut people off from their families. This is their preferred strategy. When the family is far away, it's even easier. For my brother, brainwashing was involved. I am firmly convinced that someone, even several people, had the precise task of distancing my brother from his family. Those people must have spent time denigrating me and badmouthing our whole family, in Morocco and in France alike.

At the same time I unintentionally committed a basic error by sending Zacarias pamphlets warning against Wahhabism. His 'new acquaintances' were quick to see the critical spirit that I could induce in their new recruit. Zacarias did not just wake up one day and decide that I was a 'heathen'. The thoughts he expressed to our sister were the culmination of a long process of denigration. Zacarias had probably told them about his family. The people manipulating him were quick to realize that it wasn't his sister and his mother who represented any real danger. There was an urgent need, however, to separate him from me, a Sunni. For Zacarias also told our sister, after he had received the writings denouncing the Wahhabis, that his group had declared us heathens because we were practising *tawassul*.

There is a twofold significance here. First, that group was afraid of my influence. Zacarias's elder brother, a Sunni and in their eyes a 'heathen', risked sabotaging the process that the group had set up. Part of the Wahhabi technique involves avoiding all exchanges with the Sunnis, and demonizing them, so as to minimize the impact they can still have. They accept no dissent nor the slightest challenge to what they have to say. Secondly, it meant that, from London, that group had found ways and means of finding out about me – further proof, if any were needed, of the range and efficiency of their networks. When you manage to cut somebody off from their family and friends, you achieve real power.

For my brother, like all immigrants and visitors who passed through England, cultural uprooting played a major role in the dragooning recruiting process. Those young Muslims who headed for London knew nothing about the codes of British society. They found themselves in a foreign land not necessarily welcoming, a land where foreigners like them are tolerated as long as they don't stray too far from their community. Zacarias, as we have seen, is a French man who is not at ease with being French, and a Moroccan who can't speak Arabic. Which community does he belong to? His malaise would definitely foster a sense of belonging to the group that took him in. Lastly, the denigration of all traditional Sunnite references and authorities would help to distance him from me and rid him of all critical faculties.

This enrolment was obviously greatly helped by his total ignorance of religion. This was virgin territory: he had no references and no moral weapons with which to defend himself. In my book, this kind of brainwashing or indoctrination is much less easy with a young man who has grown up in a country with a Sunnite tradition, such as Morocco, and who already has a religious culture and has studied extremist movements.

How are new recruits approached? How did my brother have his first contact with those responsible for his transformation? In London, nothing could be easier. Until September 11th, the British government more or less put up with extremist groups expressing themselves in the street on the sole condition that they respected British institutions. And today, outside certain mosques in London, every Friday you can still come across fanatics who, for example, are allowed to justify loud and clear the attacks of September 11th. As long as they don't say anything against Britain. The British call this 'freedom of speech'... Some London mosques are also renowned for the extremist sermons of their imam, especially the Finsbury Park Mosque.

And then, like all sects, these movements seem to have something irresistibly generous about them. This generosity often involves charitable organizations set up by the sects with the help of grants from abroad. Zacarias, who sometimes went hungry, told me, at the time when he was hanging out with Algerian immigrants, that they were offered meals at the mosques. What easier way to attract someone who is hungry than with a wholesome plateful of food?

The sermons given by extremist imams are as effective as they are among young people at a loose end because they exacerbate their sense of identity: they fill their heads with the suffering of Muslim people. The believer listening to this kind of sermon feels like a potential victim. All the more so because of the constant references to the massacres in Chechnya, Palestine and Algeria (which, needless to say, in the early stages, were not the work of the Armed Islamic Group). In the case of Zacarias, that particular antenna was already sensitive before he left France. It just needed honing and manipulating. In those sermons, there is, for example, no distinction made between the suffering of the Palestinian people and that of the Algerian people. Yet the pain of the Algerian having his throat cut by his neighbour has nothing to do with the pain of the Palestinian buried alive beneath his house by an Israeli tank. It is the mixed-message technique which leads both to the exacerbation of the identity problem and to a desire to be militant and struggle against injustice. Added to this is a regular and systematic reminder of all the feelings of exclusion of which the recruit might have been victim, in France and in England alike. This gives rise to a sense of pain, and when you suffer you reflect less. It is hard to take a step back to analyse the situation in the cold light of day.

Extremists also know how to cultivate people's weaknesses, the better to manipulate them. One of these major weaknesses is pride. Nowadays it is easy to cultivate among those with a ready ear the sense of belonging to a religious and intellectual elite, and the sweet certainty of thus being 'above' mere mortals. Language, here, is a valuable tool for extremists. It is also designed to bolster group identity. Wahhabis have a vocabulary all their own, which is easy to identify and designed to forge a sense of oneness and membership. All those who are not like them are *kouffar*, heathens. Their leaders are *khalifes* or 'emirs'. Warriors are called '*mujahideen*'. These terms do indeed exist in Muslim law, but the Wahhabis give them their own spin.

After several months spent usually exclusively within these groups, the young recruit is ripe for action. This at least is what he is told. This mysterious 'action' is presented to him as a duty and an honour. He becomes 'eligible' to go abroad. Depending on how ready he is, he may be directly invited to 'go for training' in a camp. Or else to go abroad 'in order to contact Muslims from other countries': for example, Muslims from Pakistan. Once on the spot, he is put up in a camp 'to see how things are'. Once in the camp, it is easy, as in any sect, to make him lose his bearings. First of all he is put through athletic training, and then training in weapon handling. These are intensive exercises. He is always being set challenges that are increasingly difficult to meet. The young recruit is not well fed. He gradually becomes exhausted. He never manages to completely come up with what is being asked of him. After several weeks or months, he gets the feeling that he's not capable of doing what is expected of him. He experiences a feeling of embarrassment and malaise. In his own eyes, he is completely belittled: he feels guilty because he is incompetent. And yet he is told over and over again that others before him have succeeded and gone on to 'great things'...

At this stage there are two possible scenarios. Either the

young recruit feels highly unmotivated, but deep down he retains his survival instinct. This type of recruit will find ways and means (and some with the help of their embassies) to go back to his country of origin, which thus retrieves a young man who is broken and disgusted, but most of the time rid of this ideology. I have collected accounts which describe the path taken by former 'recruits' such as these. Or he carries on. And if he carries on, it is to the bitter end... Because *incompetent*, the only thing he can do to help the cause is to give his life to it. And this will also prove to others that, at the end, he met their expectations.

He is now ripe for suicide. Wahhabi and Qotbist leaders announce here, there and everywhere, including on the al-Jazeera television channel, with large audiences in Arab countries, that suicide committed during an attack or an assassination is not a suicide, whereas God says in the Koran An-nisa', verse 29: 'Do not kill yourself, Allah is merciful to you.' In addition, Prophet Muhammad said, 'He who kills himself with some thing, shall be chastized with that same thing in hell', a *hadith*[4] recounted by Al-Bukhari. It is thus quite clear that Islam forbids suicide and advocates fairness. Proof lies in these words quoted in the Koran: 'Oh, you who believe, be upright for Allah's sake, bearers of witness with justice; and let not hatred of a people incite you not to act equitably. Be just; that is nearer to observance of duty. And keep your duty to Allah. Surely Allah is aware of what you do.'[5]

It was after talking things over with my sister Jamila, and then with Sheik As-Siddiq Al-Ghoumari in Tangier, that I became quite certain that my brother was in serious trouble. What could I do about it? My options were all the more limited because Zacarias wasn't living close to me. I didn't know who his friends and acquaintances were in England. The only possible avenue open to me was not to cut my links with him, in the hope that he would outgrow this phase. But I was wasting my time, because Zacarias himself broke off contact with me. In 1996, when I got back from Morocco, I didn't know where he was. Nor did my sister. He phoned her now and then, and he sometimes called our mother. But his phone calls became ever rarer, and he never answered their questions. He just said to them: 'I'm fine. I can't tell you where I am.' Was he still London? Nobody knew.

For me, all this pointed to only one thing: over the years, the sect had won. It had managed to persuade him to cut his family ties. I don't know exactly when Zacarias started to be in touch with the Wahhabis. Even today, despite everything I've read or heard about it, it's still a great mystery for me. How can someone so open, so communicative and warm, how can someone ambitious, so involved in working towards his degrees, and so keen to get away from an underprivileged social environment, how can someone like him let himself be swallowed up by such scum? How come it worked with him?

Sometimes, when I get up in the morning, I'm still dumbfounded when I think about him. It seems unreal to me. I say to myself: 'How is it possible?' Yes, my brother does have his weaknesses, but he also has great inner strength. He proved as much, first of all, by putting up with what he had to endure in his childhood, and then by never giving up his studies and never losing sight of his goal. These thoughts now make me very pessimistic because I'm at least convinced of one thing: if it worked with my brother, it can work with plenty of other young people.

As for my own role in this sad turn of events, I would say that I was always one step behind him. I didn't see or hear anything. I had to wait until 1996 and that discussion with my sister to realize that Zacarias was in such a bad way. But their conversation dated from the year before, and at that time my brother had already cut himself off from me. What should I have done? Perhaps, seeing him change and become so introspective and silent, I should have been more alarmed. I could have suspected drugs or a sect, but I didn't. Just one thing concerned me, patching up the shortcomings in our family, and providing him with a stable and affectionate environment. I definitely didn't ask myself the right questions. After my sister talked to me, the pieces of the jigsaw suddenly came together: gestures, startling words and silences. All of a sudden everything was so clear. But it was too late.

Am I in a position to give advice to families who may be affected by this type of indoctrination? To North African families I can only advise them to make sure that their children have the foundations of religious culture. Knowledge is the only possible weapon in the face of ideologies of terror. Society can have plenty of influence over the way a human being evolves. But it cannot influence the family circle. The family must be the most solid of anchors for any young person. Our own family environment was particularly unsettling. Other people have childhoods and adolescences that are even worse – of this I am well aware. But those who emerge unscathed are rare exceptions. All four of us brothers and sisters have been affected. Today, my sisters Nadia and Jamila are traumatized. My brother Zacarias stands accused of a horrendous crime, and is rotting in an American prison. If there is any point in 'giving advice' to society, I would ask society to learn to fight racial discrimination and social exclusion. Every citizen must rally to this struggle.

What is surprising is that certain people who have access to the media are known to use double-speak; they do not denounce Wahhabi ideologists such as Muhammad ibn Abd al-Wahhâb, Ibn Baz and Al-Outhaymine, and the Muslim Brotherhood ideologists: Sayyid Qotb, Al-Mawdoudi and Al-Qaradawi. For it is too easy to condemn attacks and assassinations, and at the same time to use in your dialectic arguments which allow attacks and assassinations. People of good will must be united in denouncing and ostracizing from society those who espouse the destructive ideology of these terrorist movements. Politicians must make sure that we do not ourselves become the executioners' accomplices, be it out of ignorance or mere laxity.

8

ZACARIAS IS NOT A ONE-OFF CASE

At this juncture I would like to describe briefly what happened to Xavier, one of my classmates.

I met Xavier in Perpignan. I'd just moved up into the second year of advanced vocational training and he was starting his first year. I was twenty-three, he about twenty. He'd came from Montpellier. He was a tall, strapping young man, an impressive six-foot-one and well built with it. Girls found his smile seductive. He was as kind as he was physically striking. Above all, Xavier had a very subtle wit and his cheerfulness was contagious. I could quite literally laugh until I cried when I was with him. When he was among us at the evening meals we would make in our digs, you could be sure of having a good time. Xavier had a way of telling stories that made us laugh so hard we couldn't catch our breath. For him, nothing was ever dramatic. He was refined, lively and fun. I had been living in Perpignan long enough to have a pretty full address book. There were boys and girls in it, and the girls' list particularly interested Xavier. He was so likeable that we very quickly became inseparable.

That guy had 'something'. It was difficult to define, perhaps it was just charm. He had a way of being that meant that you forgave him many things. He was fun and he was funny. He joked all the time. And even when he exaggerated, he did it with such ingenuousness that everybody cracked up. One day he drove Fouzia, Zacarias and me to Montpellier. We were looking for a parking space. A driver just ahead of us with a big car found a slot, leisurely pulled up beside the car ahead, switched on his right indicator, started to reverse... and stopped dead. Xavier had already parked our car in the spot, and we were getting out – the guy hadn't even noticed. Dumbfounded, he wound down his window to ball us out, but Xavier was one step ahead of him and, with a beaming smile, said: 'So sorry. I didn't see you!' Never mind that the guy was driving a monster four-wheel drive. Voices were raised, but Xavier laughed in such a delightful way that the man started laughing too. That's Xavier for you.

But there was something else, something more profound that also bound us together: we both knew how painful life could be. Xavier shared one particular thing in common with me, as he did with Zac, whom he would get to know through student circles: because he was black he *knew*, in his bones, what the word 'racism' meant. What's more, we had practically the same skin colour. There was no need to discuss it; we both knew perfectly well what the other could experience and feel in that respect. Xavier, who was from Africa, had kept the habit of calling Whites 'toubabs'. Sometimes, with a bitter irony, he would say: 'Toubabs really like their house nigger, the one who makes them laugh...'

Xavier, other friends and I would spend the year partying. At the end of the academic year I left Perpignan, but I didn't leave Xavier. For me he was a real friend. I was very fond of him. He was incredibly generous.

A year later, when Xavier finished his diploma course, Zacarias had been in England for several months. He came back to France regularly, and because Xavier and I were still seeing a lot of each other my brother and he often crossed paths. Zacarias told Xavier, as well as other friends, how he'd managed to get on to an interesting university course, just the way he had wanted. And he told them how, at the end of that course, he would obtain a Master of International Business (MIB). For his friends from class, that was like an advanced business school with a little bit extra – a degree obtained in England looks good on your CV. And some of the friends who listened to him felt tempted. Zacarias told Xavier he could help him out to start with. He now knew London well, along with all the crucial ins and outs to get by. He also knew how to prepare for the entrance exam for the MIB, because he had successfully done it. Anyway, Zac was a reliable guy, a friend you could count on.

Xavier thought about those new prospects and made up his mind. In 1993, he and a classmate went to see Zacarias in London. What happened then? Hartium told me nothing special happened to begin with. Xavier passed his entrance exam for the MIB and attended his classes. So it had worked out for him. He would come back to France more or less when Zacarias did. He regularly went to see his family, especially his mother, to whom he was very attached. And he would see us, and other friends. He also told us about a British society that was to say the least double-edged; on the surface very tolerant, because you came across every nationality over there. But in reality, he said, it was based on each community living in their own ghetto. The segregation between Blacks and Whites seemed to him much more marked than it was in France. When he came back he was, as ever, fun and funny, and much appreciated by everybody. He spent most of his time with Zacarias. One summer they went on holiday together to Senegal.

In January 1995 I saw Xavier for the last time. We spent several evenings together with my wife. I still have photos of one evening. One of them shows him sitting on our bed, in our little apartment. In the photo he has very short hair and he is smiling broadly into the camera. He has a cigarette in his right hand. In another photo he is sprawled across the bed, roaring with laughter, head down, eyes all creased, he is

laughing so hard. Xavier had just told us that he had
converted to Islam. But he didn't seem to be a practising
Muslim, and he didn't pray. His behaviour was just the same.
He talked to me about the Regent's Park Mosque, and told me
proudly that he had shared a couscous there with Yusuf Islam,
the ex-singer formerly known as Cat Stevens. Then he
returned to England to continue his studies and I never saw
him again.

Zacarias, for his part, came to France in the early summer.
He announced to me that he had got his Master of International Business degree. When he went back to London, it
was to pick up his degree. I went with him to Montpellier
airport, I was proud of him because, despite all the problems
he'd had, he'd achieved his goal. I didn't know at that time that
that was the last time I would see my brother. I would not see
him again until after September 11th, through the media...

It was during the summer of 1996, on our return from
Morocco, that I noticed a marked change in Xavier. I had just
realized that my brother had been recruited by the Wahhabis,
when I discovered to my amazement that Xavier too had
adopted their arguments. What my Montpellier friends then
told me left me dumbfounded. Xavier had arrived, introduced
himself as my friend, and tried to get his message across – at
the very same time, and with the very same arguments, as
Zacarias in the Narbonne mosque. The coincidence was more
than disturbing. I drew the conclusion that the Wahhabis had
once again succeeded in indoctrinating a new convert. I was
sincerely upset for him. Xavier's brother, whom I met in
Montpellier on several occasions, told me that he was also
very worried. He didn't understand what was happening. He
told me that Xavier had told them he had gone to Kuwait with
Zacarias, apparently to learn religion. 'Learn religion! Learn
Wahhabism, more like!' I said to him. And I explained to him
what that movement is. I knew that in Kuwait there were very
important establishments teaching Wahhabism. The fact was,

his brother told me, that they had all gradually seen Xavier changing as well. But because they didn't know anything about Islam, they thought for a long time that it was to do with his new conversion, and that all Muslims behaved like that. When they realized that his behaviour was abnormal, and the change in him far too abrupt, it was, once again, too late.

And I offered that brother, who was as devastated as I was, the only advice that seemed to me to be realistic: not to burn his bridges with Xavier, to try to keep a connection, even if he and I felt so helpless in front of such changes. We just didn't understand how those two boys, both of them lovers of life, could have let themselves be indoctrinated like that. We parted telling each other that all that was perhaps just the craziness of youth, and it would pass. From that day on, Zacarias didn't call me any more and never came to see me – a deafening silence. I didn't understand how my younger brother had ended up finding it acceptable to strike us out of his life. It hurt me. I had always thought that our shared years of suffering had woven indestructible bonds. It was as if a part of me had been amputated. I had to suffer in silence. There is one thing that doesn't fail to heighten my distress: throughout all those years of absence, nobody bothered to find out what had become of Zacarias. I had the feeling of being the only person to remember him.

What really is this Wahhabism which breaks up families? I have read in textbooks and history books about the bloody and destructive consequences of Wahhabism and the ideology of the Muslim Brotherhood. But for me those are just words. In my gut, and in my heart, through these pangs of anguish which awake me at night, I understand that the reality behind that ideology is suffering and injustice. From now on, whenever I meet a young or a not-so-young person who engages me in a sectarian arguments, I try to guide that person back to more moderate thinking, backed up by proof and argument. And if necessary, I share my experience with him. I describe how extremism has taken my brother away. I think I've understood that it's important not to give a free rein to Wahhabis and the Muslim Brotherhood. So I'm involved in preventive work. Now I can clearly see the relevance of the warnings of the imam at the At-Tawba Mosque against extremist movements. In 1992 I started to go to the Association of Islamic Welfare Projects in France, whose members were the only people to have warned me against the danger of the Wahhabis.

One day in the year 2000 I was summoned by the Montpellier police. A policeman ushered me into an office and asked me to sit down. With no further ado, and in complete silence, they showed me a colour photocopy of a page from a website. On that page, there was an article about the war in Chechnya with three colour photos: three photos of Xavier. In the first photo, taken outdoors, he was standing behind two other soldiers, wearing a military uniform and a dark cap pulled down around his ears. He was smiling at the camera with the forefinger of his right hand raised. The second photo showed him sideways on, again in a military uniform. He had a thin moustache and a long beard. His head was shaved. He wasn't smiling any more but holding his chin in his hand, apparently deep in thought. In the last photo, he was lying down alongside other men, with a blanket pulled up over him. His right leg was covered in blood. His eyes were closed. He looked as if he was asleep, and not in pain. The photo had a caption, and the words leaped out at me, searing my eyes: 'Massoud Al-Benin, born in France, lived in London, died in Chechnya.'

Xavier. The article accompanying the photo announced his death on 12 April 2000. I read it, understanding nothing, full of disbelief. I felt like crying, tears welled up, but I managed not to break down in front of the policemen, who hadn't exactly handled me with kid gloves. They asked me if I knew where my brother was. 'The French government,' they told me, 'would like to warn French nationals about the risks they are taking.' So they obviously thought that my brother was with Xavier, in Chechnya, or going there soon. I didn't know what to think any more. I expected the worst but, deep down inside me, I hoped for the best.

Every day after that I found myself expecting to hear that my brother was dead. You never get used to such ideas. I also told myself that he had possibly died already in some far-flung corner of the world and that I would never know about it. Now I have a better understanding of the determination of families of people who have disappeared to want to know the truth about the fate of their nearest and dearest. I lived with this expectation until the tragedy of September 11th.

9

THE MEDIA STORM

On September 11th 2001 I was in class with my students. And we watched live, on television, the second aeroplane as it crashed and exploded in one of the World Trade Center towers. We were stunned by those terrifying images. There was an instant flood of questions: Who? Why? How could it be possible? In the United States! At that particular moment we imagined perhaps tens of thousands of deaths. All those people who had set off that morning saying 'See you tonight' to their families. They would never see them again. The two towers collapsed one after the other and the vision of horror worsened. I knew that there were people of all nationalities and all religions in the Twin Towers. Once again, the victims were civilians.

Driving back to Montpellier, I learned that a certain 'Franco-Algerian Zacarias Moussaoui' might be involved. The impact of those images had me feeling immediately concerned. I instantly felt close to all that pain. But when I heard that announcement, I felt dizzy. I had the impression of teetering into the void, into somewhere unknown that I knew to be tragic. I had a hunch that I was about to be crushed. I was summoned by the police on 14 September, and they told me about Zacarias's situation: he had been in prison since 16 August and an FBI suspect. When I left the police station I felt completely shattered. For the past few years I'd been expecting the worst, but hanging on to a sliver of hope. I thought about my mother and sisters. How were they living through this disaster? Fouzia and I thought about going to see them. We thought that our pain might perhaps bring us all together again. I had to get back to work.

The first articles about Zacarias Moussaoui started to appear. That was the beginning of the slander and libel about my wife and me. They said that I myself was a member of the Muslim Brotherhood. They said my brother and I were terrorists, me a sleeper, him active. My wife was also allegedly a former Muslim Brotherhood member and responsible for Zacarias's downward spiral. But there were more surprises in store. Some articles reported insulting comments about Fouzia: 'Cancer had entered our house', and 'I didn't know that I'd let the wolf into the fold.' And as if it were necessary to add insult to all this injury, certain papers said that my mother was the author of these remarks… Fouzia and I were shocked and alarmed. We just couldn't believe it. I didn't understand anything any more. I couldn't imagine that my mother would take advantage of the situation to get her own back. I was tired of the family rows and had kept my distance, hoping that time would heal those wounds and enable us to come together again one day.

But no such luck. Just violence, lies, libel and people stooping to anything. That's what I was finding in the papers and that's what was being attributed to my mother. I'd never talked about those family rows. Anyone can understand that it's not nice to hear bad things said about yourself, and in the case of Fouzia and myself it was the entire international press that was echoing these libellous accusations. Those lies were serious because they had to do with a real tragedy, and several thousand deaths. Certain people had no respect for our dignity as human beings. At school, a colleague thrust an article before my eyes in which it was written that I was close to the Muslim Brotherhood movement. And he said to me: 'I want some explanations.' People would look away when I walked by, and there was silence when I walked into the teachers' common room. Some colleagues suddenly seemed very busy, and gradually the room would empty out. Everybody said they had things to do. I was totally distraught, because I felt that the press campaign might have catastrophic consequences for my job. I'd been working in the state education system for twelve years, and the last six teaching electrical engineering, as an assistant teacher. This meant that I didn't have tenure. And at every new school year I am assigned to a different school. It would be easy not to give me any post at all.

When the events of September 11th shook the face of the earth, I had been working for two weeks at the vocational school in Mende. So my new colleagues had hardly had time to get to know me. Then all of a sudden they were seeing my name in the press. From one day to the next, they found themselves working side by side with the brother of a presumed terrorist linked to the carnage of September 11th. Many of my teacher colleagues avoided the subject. When I was present they talked about hobbies and cooking. The whole world was asking questions about that tragedy, and they went to great pains not to broach the issue in my presence. Maybe some of them weren't sure how to talk about it with me. Maybe they were afraid of going too far in their conclusions, or maybe they had believed the lies about me and saw me as a latent terrorist. I plucked up courage and decided to deal with the situation. I would talk to all those people of good will. I would certainly not isolate myself. I would take the initiative and bring my colleagues together and explain candidly to them what was going on.

I did this during the ten o'clock coffee break in the common room. All the teaching staff were there. In a stony silence, I told them what I thought about it all. I told them I was a Muslim and that I in no way espoused an ideology of terror and destruction. I explained to them that all those newspapers had been lying and that I had never had any connections with any terrorists. A colleague spoke out sufficiently loudly so that everybody could hear: 'Don't worry. As far as I'm concerned, I believe you, not the papers.' Many of them told me how deeply my situation was exercising them. The most recurrent questions were: Where were the ethics and morality in all this? Where was the human aspect? On the days that followed, lots of newspapers, and radio and television reports continued to bombard their public with information, true or false. My colleagues didn't know what to think. I got the impression that they too felt overtaken by events.

On the Thursday, I went back to Montpellier. It was a two-and-a-half-hour drive, so I had plenty of time to think. I was quite sure I should reply to all those lies and all that libel. But how? With whom? Who would agree to hear me out? I didn't know how, but I knew I had to do something. I reached Montpellier at ten in the evening. A friend who was devastated by what he'd been reading in the newspapers had given me the press cuttings he had kept for me. Journalists were waiting for me – Canal+, France 2, TF1. They wanted an interview. I felt tremendous pressure, heightened by everything I'd read in those cuttings. I was tired after my drive, but now I felt angry. My disappointment ran deep. I still couldn't believe that my mother had gone so far as to unjustly accuse my wife and myself of such serious things in such a terrifying context. Yes, spiritual instruction does teach us that it's better to be the victim than the oppressor. But being the victim of injustice leaves a bitter taste in the mouth. Fouzia and I jointly decided to state our case. But we decided not to answer the libellous accusations, either by way of the media or in the courts. In this tragic situation, we thought it was far more useful to warn against generalizations that lump

Muslims and terrorists together.

I sought to protect what was left of my privacy: my home. So I asked the imam if I could use the mosque to conduct interviews with the journalists. He agreed. As it so happened, on 9 September the mosque had taken part in a forum of associations. Several hundred of them had presented their activities and their goals. The forum lasted all day and filled a whole neighbourhood of Montpellier. So I had access to the information panels about Muslim beliefs, introducing the principles of Islam, retracing the historical and geographical spread of Muslims throughout the world, and, in particular, panels showing the range of architecture that exists in the Muslim world. The point was to show that Islam builds and does not destroy, with an altogether striking parallel between Roman architecture and Arabic-Muslim architecture through-out the world. What came across was that local people had accepted and incorporated Islam in their own architectural tradition. There were also panels explaining why the principles of Islam are opposed to the Wahhabi and Qotbist ideologies.

Several tables also described the importance of training and learning in the foundations of religion for all Muslims, and the Sunnite attachment to spirituality – in particular, Sufi practice.[1] And the importance of great masters of the science of the purification of the heart, such as Abu Bakr, Omar Outhman and the fourth caliph, Imam Ali (may it please Allah), and even the great saints such as Al-Djunayd and Ahmad Ar-Rifaï. Another panel also showed the translation of the Friday discourses read out in the mosque.

Until two in the morning, I explained my brother's story to a succession of journalists. I showed them the information tables and the pamphlets warning against terrorism and extremism, which had been published in the mosque for years. I told them that I hadn't seen my brother since 1995, that I hadn't been passive and inactive, that, on the contrary,

I had made my contribution to various social and cultural activities. I tried to get them to understand and to point out to them that the task of warning against extremism is a day-to-day task, precise and methodical but vital and something that can't be ignored. This, moreover, was why my wife and I felt cheated and scorned, as if people wanted to deny our opinions by labelling us as extremists and fanatics. With the newspapers dragging our names into the mud, I felt that my social involvement and my work with clubs was being dismissed.

Some of the people who came to meet me didn't just want to know about the life of the alleged terrorist Zacarias Moussaoui; they were also keen to meet the brother who was supposed to share the same ideas, and to see his wife, who was probably the brains behind the whole thing... This, needless to say, did not make for easy first contacts with the press. Several journalists told me, after they had turned up, that they had come suspicious, wary and sometimes even worried. One of them, a woman, had been paralysed with fear. After talking for twenty minutes, she phoned her husband to tell him she was all right and that we were normal people, so there was no need for him to worry. What exactly were they expecting?

I realized that the mosque was totally misunderstood as a place of worship. With a few rare exceptions, most of those journalists had never set foot inside a mosque, and they felt visibly ill at ease in it. There was a lot of confusion. Some thought they didn't have the right to go inside. That bothered me, because I realized that plenty of journalists knew nothing at all about their country's second most important religion. I even wondered if some of them weren't being ignorant on purpose, they had such a glaring lack of culture. For some, there's something 'shady' about a Muslim praying five times a day: he had to be a fundamentalist or on the way to becoming one. They saw the Muslim as fatalistic and rigid, with a cumbersome, not to say eccentric religious practice. For some, it was a bit as if all Muslims were potential extremists, at least until proven to the contrary.

My close friends and my family were all deeply shocked by what they were reading in the press. I wouldn't wish this kind of traumatizing experience on anyone. For me, a professional journalist is someone who gets out there, investigates, double-checks his information and confirms it through different sources. He's certainly not someone who's content with just one side of a story. Luckily, my wife, friends and the imam of the mosque were there to back me up.

Three weeks had gone by since September 11th. The media storm turned into a hurricane: *Le Monde, Le Parisien, Le Figaro, Libération, France Soir, Le Progrès de Lyon, L'Indépendent de Perpignan, Le Midi Libre, L'Express, Le Point, VSD, Paris Match, Courrier International, Le Nouvel Observateur, La Gazette de Montpellier, Le Journal du Dimanche, Al-Hayat* (an Arab newspaper published in London), *NRC Handelsblad* (a Dutch newspaper), *Le Maroc International Hebdo, The Times, The Sunday Times,* TFI, France 2, France 3, La Cinquième, M6, LCI, CBS News, MTV Info and AM (German TV stations), NetWORK (a Dutch channel), ABC, Channel 4, CNN, NHK (a Japanese channel), an Australian public service channel, France Info, Radio France International, RMC, , the Dow Jones agency...

The TV crews usually consisted of a journalist, a sound recordist and a cameraman. Press crews had a journalist and a photographer. Sometimes the same channel sent several crews. In the mad rush and spontaneity of it all, Fouzia and I shared the various tasks. Fouzia dealt with looking over what was in the press, rights of reply and any follow-up there might be (no media published any denials), and she also organized my appointments. The imam at the mosque received journalists, answered their questions and spent hours explaining to them how, from a religious standpoint, the terror ideology had no foundations. In the mosque, journalists were given tea and cakes, and the people at the reception desks tirelessly answered the ever-ringing phone. They kept the journalists company and made them wait their turn. Everybody was hospitable.

Yet some journalists left quite a lot to be desired when it came to being tactful, and certainly didn't beat about the bush. One journalist asked me: 'Is it true that you're a fundamentalist?' Was he hoping I'd say 'Yes'? Some, displeased that I hadn't granted them an interview, would go into a huddle with their colleagues and portray me as an extremist. Others used hidden cameras even though the mosque was open to them and nobody was hiding anything. On the other hand, others tried to learn and understand things, taking the trouble to take a close look both at the task of warning against extremism and at the education and instruction going on in the mosque. I also came across some journalists who did their job with professionalism and humanity.

There was nothing smug about the way they went about their work. Others, with fewer scruples, wrote articles as if they had met me, whereas they hadn't even left their desks or taken the trouble to phone me. And when I expressed outrage at that practice, they told me it was par for the course. Journalists often work from articles that have already been published, and these are the sole 'sources' they use to write their piece. They also explained to me that for them it wasn't surprising to find the same lies cropping up in different newspapers, because local correspondents often freelance for several papers at the same time. They call this the 'snowball' effect. So, in my case, the correspondent of a local paper went to interview my mother and took down what she had to say in exchange for cash. He published an article that was in turn taken up by another local correspondent who worked for several local and national newspapers. This information was then taken up by international press agencies. And that's how I got to be labelled an extremist, a fanatic and a dormant terrorist. People even made my wife Fouzia responsible for Zacarias being brainwashed and recruited, and me too: 'It all just has to be a woman's fault!' Fouzia's image in the papers was a caricature verging on racism: it was the image of an intellectually limited woman, who advocated that men shouldn't do the washing-up. In another context we might have laughed it off, we found it so ridiculous. Psychologically, it was very hard. First, because Fouzia and I felt totally denied as human beings. The thoughts people attributed to us were the very opposite of our values, our convictions and our moral codes. We were the victims of the sweeping generalization whereby everyone conspired to make 'Muslim' synonymous with 'terrorist'.

My wife and I weren't the only ones to have been traumatized. In the great media stampede, the congregation at the mosque wavered between indignation – sections of the press denigrated their religion – and fear. They were in fact afraid of reprisals against the mosque. In the United States, a Sikh had been murdered because he'd been taken for a Muslim, because of his beard and the turban on his head. Insulting and threatening death letters were sent to the mosque. One day a giant of a man turned up there asking to see me. I wasn't around, so he left a message: 'Tell Abd Samad that he had better watch what he says or he might have problems.' And he drove off at the wheel of his red four-wheel drive with British plates. Apparently, I was getting up certain people's noses. Not only was the reputation being given me a libellous one, but in addition it was dangerous for my wife, for me, and for mosques and Muslims in general.

We eventually realized that certain journalists weren't interested in what we had to say; what's more, our arguments disturbed them. It would all be so much more thrilling if we really were extremists – and above all, the story would sell better. In this dreadful story, they saw a kind of crime novel and made monsters of the characters involved. Despite all these upheavals, I tried to stay cool, calm and collected, day after day. It didn't stop for three months. Then the breaker would became a wavelet, but before long it would start all over again – every time anyone talked about my brother, or his silence, or the legal proceedings now under way.

Sometime later, in a lull, a journalist from a weekly asked me to help him write an article. I spent hours working with him. He never asked if he could get in touch with Fouzia. When the article appeared all I found in it was malicious gossip and lies about my wife. Once again, what was said about her was attributed to my mother. Fouzia observed: 'This type of attitude raises three questions: if it's acceptable to write this kind of article because I'm a Muslim, then it shows intolerance; if it's because I'm Moroccan, then it shows racism; and if it's because I'm a woman, then it shows sexism and misogyny.' For me, that guy was a stupid idiot who used the pain and blindness of one woman to hurt another woman.

10

By Way of Conclusion

The sacred religious writings in the Holy Koran teach justice and moderation. The wisdom of nations must be learned mutually among peoples. Thus, we read in the Koran the Word of Allah, which says: 'O mankind, surely We have created you from a male and a female, and made you tribes and families that you may know each other. Surely the noblest of you with Allah is the most dutiful of you.'[1] And further: 'And let not hatred of a people – because they hindered you from the Sacred Mosque – incite you to transgress. And help one another in righteousness and piety and help not one another in sin and aggression.'[2] God orders us to be a community of justice, fairness and the happy medium. God says this in the Holy Koran: 'And thus We have made you an exalted nation that you may be the bearers of witness to the people and [that] the messenger may be a bearer of witness to you.'[3]

The Koran also teaches us to be concerned with the best works, goodness, charity and fairness to obtain the elevation of the soul: 'And everyone has a goal to which he turns [himself], so vie with one another in good works.'[4] The Koran teaches us to discuss in a tolerant manner: 'Call to the way of thy Lord with wisdom and goodly exhortation, and argue with them in the best manner.'[5] It teaches us to prefer indulgence while giving the right to apply justice: 'And if you take your turn, then punish with the like of that with which you were afflicted. But if you show patience, it is certainly best for the patient.'[6] These are the true precepts of Muslim religious education.

What is the current situation with young Muslim people in France? Looking back over my life to date, and my brother's, I can identify with those hundreds of thousands of young people: lack of parental authority, a difficult childhood, poor education without any goals and without religious references, but rather awash in ignorance about the cultural heritage of our countries of origin, and exclusion everywhere you look. Nowadays, I wonder if I'm not a survivor. Could I too have been ensnared, in the way my brother was, by extremist groups? Thank the Lord that the people who introduced me to Islam taught me that attachment to religion means an adherence to moderation. Prophet Muhammad said: 'Guard against exaggeration in matters of religion.'[7]

The more the young Muslim turns his back on religion, the more vulnerable he is. Nowadays the danger of false religious people, dealing in exclusion and extremism, lies in wait for us everywhere. The only bulwarks I know reside in traditional religious culture, in parental support and presence and in a real policy of struggle against all forms of exclusion, free of demagogy and political cant.

EPILOGUE

WHO PAYS THE PRICE?

The victims of attacks are of all nationalities, all origins, all skin colours and all religions, be it in Egypt, Algeria or New York. Then there are the families of victims who survive the death of a loved one, and there are the friends of those who have disappeared who are also traumatized by this barbarity.

There are Muslims the world over who are under suspicion and being wrongly accused. Muslims are the victims of a sweeping generalization: 'Islam equals terrorism.' There is the Islam which people attempt to discredit and which is nevertheless innocent of all this fanaticism and all this terror. There are also the families of all those implicated and suspected of being involved in the attacks, families who are all at sea, lamenting their disarray, their pain and their incomprehension in the face of this tragedy. They would like to think that it is a nightmare and yet all this is very real. Every day, all these victims experience suffering and sadness.

And, lastly, a major victim: the just causes of all those oppressed and crushed Muslim peoples. Those Afghans, Chechens and Bosnians, who see themselves being recuperated by international Wahhabism. To survive they stumble from wars of liberation and resistance into extremist traps. Wahhabi fanatics, supported by brainwashed young people through a Qotbist doctrine of massive excommunication, monopolize and engulf just causes. They have financial wealth and weaponry worthy of powerful states. Wahhabis make the most of war to infiltrate local populations and in particular the youth they are so keen to indoctrinate. From this nursery, they will pluck the most fanatical and use them as weapons of destruction everywhere in the world. And when they start to attack civilians and provoke the enemy, they shake up all the dignitaries in those populations and relegate them to the background. The Wahhabis whttle away what prestige they do have and force them out. This hostage-taking has political and financial ends, with foreign powers as the beneficiaries. To achieve their goal, they first attack religious traditions, doing away with them and then suppressing the rampart of moderate and tolerant religious principles, around which Muslim populations rally. Secondly, they physically attack the religious and political references of these populations. They even go so far as to organize terror by way of despicable attacks against civilians on both sides. The cards are shuffled and there is complete confusion. The earliest defenders of just causes are now stripped of their arguments. They have become the victims of those who have taken their causes hostage.

In France, various sources of information estimate the number of young people enrolled annually in bin Laden's training camps at between eighty and three hundred. This means that between eighty and three hundred families are affected. So these are not isolated cases, but rather a blight on society. French, Americans, Franco-Moroccans, Franco-Algerians, Australians, Belgians, Yemenis, Lebanese, Egyptians… they come from many different countries, so we are facing a problem of international scope.

If we are sincerely interested in bringing this spiral of terror to an end, we cannot skim over a certain number of unsettling questions. Why do some countries make it easy for the Wahhabis and parties like the Muslim Brotherhood to spread their propaganda? The careers of all those young people allegedly implicated in the attacks passed by way of Great Britain. Why have the British authorities been so lax? It is well known to one and all that American secret services supported bin Laden for twenty years. How could they be unaware of the dangers represented by that? Why, in France, do the authorities still deal with organizations and individuals who lay claim to ideologies based on terror?

Do we also need our own September 11th to finally open our eyes?

REFERENCES

A Note from the Editor of the French Edition

1. Frédéric Chambon, 'Entre New York et Narbonne, l'échange épistolaire entre Aïcha et Zacarias Moussaoui', *Le Monde*, 18 November 2001. ['Between New York and Narbonne, letters written to each other by Aïcha and Zacarias Moussaoui'].

2. Jean-Marie Pontaut and Éric Pelletier, 'Révélations sur les réseaux Bin Laden' ['Revelations about the bin Laden networks'], *L'Express*, 13 June 2002.

3. Eric Leser, 'La police fédérale en accusation', *Le Monde*, 16–17 June 2002.

4. As the French edition of this book went to press, the trial was postponed until 2003. It has since been further postponed. No new trial date has been set.

1. A 'Family'

1. This name has been changed, as have some other names throughout the book.

2. Teenage Years: Fun Times and Frustrations

1. The French equivalent to A-levels.

3. Looking for an Identity

1. *Le Monde*, 27 September 2001.

2. Rosaries.

3. A *siwak* is a wooden twig that is used to clean your teeth. It may be from an olive or palm tree, but the best *siwaks* come from the al-'arak tree.

4. Members of a pietistic movement founded in 1927. By nature, the movement is missionary, proselytizing and radically anti-fundamentalist.

5. Sayyid Qotb, *A l'ombre du Qour'an*, Al-Hidayah Al-Islamiyah, 1988.

6. Sayyid Qotb, *Jalons sur la route de l'islam*, Imprimerie de Carthage, 1968.

7. Pillars: obligations that are part of worship, without which the worship is invalid. For example, prostration prior to praying.

8. Conditions of validity are not part of any kind of worship, but without them the worship is invalid: for example, undertaking minor ablutions before praying.

9. Yusuf Al-Qaradawi, *L'Adoration de Dieu en islam*, Arrisala.

4. UPROOTED AND CAST OUT

1. The equivalent of 380 euros.

5. ZAC'S DREAM: A PLACE IN THE SUN

1. See Chapter 3.

6. DOWN AND OUT, AND ALONE IN LONDON

1. Innovation or Bidah: a new act, in the knowledge that the Prophet hadn't practised it or spoken about it. There are two categories of new acts after the Prophet. The first involves innovations to do with uprightness: these are what have been innovated in compliance with the Koran, the Sunna, Unanimity, scholars and the tradition of companions: for example, the celebration of the birth of the Prophet. The second category involves innovations to do with errors and follies: these are what have been innovated in contradiction to the Koran, the Sunna, Unanimity, scholars and the tradition of companions.

2. Sunna: beliefs and laws revealed to Prophet Muhammad.

3. *Al-Moudjahid*, 43, June 1996.

7. THE BRAINWASHING OF ZACARIAS

1. Jurisconsults (Mutjahid scholars) are the scholars with the highest credentials, capable of interpreting the laws of Islam on points that have been subject to texts or to any previous Unanimity based on the basic writings. Some of the leading scholars are Ach-chafii, Malik, Ahmad ibnou Hambal, Abu Hanifah and their peers. Unanimity (Al-Ijam) is the consensus of Mutjahid scholars on a subject to do with Islam in any area. It is not merely the unanimous agreement of any group of Muslims or even of non-Mutjahid scholars about an issue of Islam.

2. The Qotbist party known as the Muslim Brotherhood.

3. Criminal brotherhood.

4. Hadith, or prophetic tradition: a word, fact or event recounted by the Prophet or his companions.
5. Sura 5, verse 8, Al-Maidah.

9. THE MEDIA STORM
1. Sufi: a term describing the state of pious Muslims who obey Allah in compliance with the Koran, the Hadith, Unanimity and the words of the companions of Muhammad, their hearts being detached from life on earth.

10. BY WAY OF CONCLUSION
1. Sura 49, verse 13, Al-Hujurat.
2. Sura 5, verse 2, Al-Maidah.
3. Sura 2, verse 143, Al-Baqarah.
4. Sura 2, verse 148, Al-Baqarah.
5. Sura 16, verse 125, An-Nahl.
6. Sura 16, verse 126, An-Nahl.
7. *Hadith* reported in the Sunna of Ibn Majah.